WOMEN,
CULTURE,
& POLITICS

WOMEN, CULTURE, & POLITICS

ANGELA Y. DAVIS

Vintage Books
A Division of Random House, Inc.
New York

First Vintage Books Edition, February 1990

Copyright © 1984, 1985, 1986, 1987, 1988, 1989 by Angela Y. Davis

All rights reserved under International and Pan-American Copyright Conventions. Published in the United States by Vintage Books, a division of Random House, Inc., New York, and simultaneously in Canada by Random House of Canada Limited, Toronto. Originally published, in hardcover, by Random House, Inc., New York, in 1989.

Library of Congress Cataloging-in-Publication Data
Davis, Angela Yvonne, 1944–
  Women, culture & politics / Angela Y. Davis. — 1st Vintage Books
ed.
    p.   cm.
  "Originally published in hardcover by Random House...in 1989"–
–T.p. verso.
  I SBN 978-0-679-72487-2
  1. Afro-American women.   2. Afro-Americans—Social
conditions—1975–   3. Sexism—United States.   4. Racism—United
States.   5. United States—Race relations.   6. Sexism.   7. Racism.
I. Title.   II. Title: Women, culture, and politics.
E185.86.D382   1990
305.48'896073—dc20   89-40103
                                                              CIP

Page v constitutes an extension of this copyright page.

Manufactured in the United States of America

For Nikky

Acknowledgments

Five years ago, during one of my parents' regular visits to the Bay Area, I was preparing to deliver the commencement address to Berkeley High School's graduating class. My mother remarked that since I had the habit of devoting so much of my time to the preparation of speeches, I should consider publishing them in book form. I therefore thank my mother, Sallye B. Davis, for providing the initial inspiration for this book, which during the next few years remained a seductive but unrealized idea until my close friend Nikky Finney convinced me to set aside some time to work on the project. Nikky assisted me in sifting through scores of old speeches and articles with a view to gleaning material for this collection. She read the final manuscript and helped me to formulate appropriate titles for the individual pieces. The title of the chapter on Winnie Mandela, in fact, is taken from a poem Nikky wrote on women in South Africa that was in turn inspired by the women's chant that arose out of the 1956 campaign against the pass laws: "Now that you have touched the women, you have struck a rock, you have dislodged a boulder, and you will be crushed."

Some of the ideas incorporated in the speeches reflect many hours of late-night political debates with my friend June Jordan. I thank her for her enduring friendship, and I thank her for "Poem About My Rights."

Stefanie Kelly, my teaching assistant at that time in the Women's Studies Department at San Francisco State University, spent many hours at the computer typing and editing the manuscript. I thank her for her invaluable assistance.

Finally, I am immensely grateful to my administrative assistant, Roberta Goodman, who devoted painstaking attention to every phase of this project.

Contents

Introduction

The work of the political activist inevitably involves a certain tension between the requirement that positions be taken on current issues as they arise and the desire that one's contributions will somehow survive the ravages of time. In this sense the most difficult challenge facing the activist is to respond fully to the needs of the moment and to do so in such a way that the light one attempts to shine on the present will simultaneously illuminate the future. Of course, one can never really know whether one's positions and analyses will retain their value beyond the immediacy of the moment. There is thus a certain risk—and even a measure of presumptuousness—inherent in a book such as this.

It would be remiss of me not to acknowledge the personal motivation underlying this book, for it is also an attempt to capture a few of the moments in my career as an activist over the last period that would have otherwise gone the way of all such fleeting experiences. It is an effort to retrospectively provide some continuity to a life that has been informed for almost two decades by local and global struggles for progressive social change. During the late 1960s, this involvement was the background against which I was fired from my position at the University of California, Los Angeles, because of my membership in the Communist Party and was eventually arrested on false charges of murder, kidnapping, and conspiracy. Since my acquittal in 1972, much of my life has been devoted to public speaking as I have traveled and lectured throughout this country and abroad.

Although my organizational affiliations and my interests—and thus the themes of my work, my lectures, and much of my writing—have been diverse, I have always tried, whether successfully or not, to make sure that there are connecting threads that prevent me from dissipating my energies in too many directions. I have continued to function as a National Committee member of the Communist Party, as a co-chairperson of the National Alliance Against Racist and Political Repression and as member of the executive boards of the National Political Congress of Black Women and the National Black Women's Health Project. The lectures and articles collected in this book reflect—directly or indirectly—my involvement in all these movements.

A good number of the lectures published here were delivered on college campuses. I have been astonished time and time again by the large numbers of students and community people who have continued to attend and respond positively to my lectures. During the early period of my career as a lecturer, especially in the immediate aftermath of my acquittal, I was certainly cognizant of the extent to which the media coverage of my trial and the influence of the mass movement in defense of my freedom served to attract large audiences to my speeches. Many of those who came out to hear me in those days felt very much connected to the era and to people like myself who emerged as symbols of that period's rampant political repression. I assumed, however, that with the passage of years and the inevitable fading of the media image, the public persona would eventually become a historical relic for the children born to members of my generation.

What has truly surprised me is that young people on the campuses as well as in the community—women and men, students and workers, people of all racial backgrounds, who are no longer seduced by a media image long since laid to rest, are attracted by the progressive politics associated with the campaigns with which I work. A number of years ago, activists in progressive political circles began to detect an approaching resurgence of campus activism, along with a renewed vigor of labor activism. My own experiences abundantly confirmed this prediction and indeed today, in the latter 1980s, students and workers are organizing and demonstrating against domestic expressions of racism, against U.S. collusion with apartheid and against intervention in Central America. My own work over the last two decades will have been wonderfully worthwhile if it has indeed assisted in some small measure to awaken and encourage this new activism.

ON WOMEN
AND THE PURSUIT
OF EQUALITY
AND PEACE

Let Us All
Rise Together: Radical
Perspectives on Empowerment
for Afro-American Women

The concept of empowerment is hardly new to Afro-American women. For almost a century, we have been organized in bodies that have sought collectively to develop strategies illuminating the way to economic and political power for ourselves and our communities. During the last decade of the nineteenth century, after having been repeatedly shunned by the racially homogeneous women's rights movement, Black women organized their own Club Movement. In 1895—five years after the founding of the General Federation of Women's Clubs, which consolidated a club movement reflecting concerns of middle-class White women—one hundred Black women from ten states met in the city of Boston, under the leadership of Josephine St. Pierre Ruffin, to discuss the creation of a national organi-

—Address given to the National Women's Studies Association annual conference, Spellman College, June 25, 1987. Originally published under the title "Radical Perspectives on Empowerment for Afro-American Women," *Harvard Educational Review* 25, no. 3, August 1988. Copyright 1988 by the President and Fellows of Harvard College. All rights reserved.

zation of Black women's clubs. As compared to their White counterparts, the Afro-American women issuing the call for this national club movement articulated principles that were more openly political in nature. They defined the primary function of their clubs as an ideological as well as an activist defense of Black women—and men—from the ravages of racism. When the meeting was convened, its participants emphatically declared that, unlike their White sisters, whose organizational policies were seriously tainted by racism, they envisioned their movement as one open to all women:

> Our woman's movement is woman's movement in that it is led and directed by women for the good of women and men, for the benefit of *all* humanity, which is more than any one branch or section of it. We want, we ask the active interest of our men, and, too, we are not drawing the color line; we are women, American women, as intensely interested in all that pertains to us as such as all other American women; we are not alienating or withdrawing, we are only coming to the front, willing to join any others in the same work and cordially inviting and welcoming any others to join us.[1]

The following year, the formation of the National Association of Colored Women's Clubs was announced. The motto chosen by the Association was "Lifting As We Climb."[2]

The nineteenth-century women's movement was also plagued by classism. Susan B. Anthony wondered why her outreach to working-class women on the issue of the ballot was so frequently met with indifference. She wondered why these women seemed to be much more concerned with improving their economic situation than with achieving the right to vote.³ As essential as political equality may have been to the larger campaign for women's rights, in the eyes of Afro-American and White working-class women it was not synonymous with emancipation. That the conceptualization of strategies for struggle was based on the peculiar condition of White women of the privileged classes rendered those strategies discordant with working-class women's perceptions of empowerment. It is not surprising that many of them told Ms. Anthony, "Women want bread, not the ballot."⁴ Eventually, of course, working-class White women, and Afro-American women as well, reconceptualized this struggle, defining the vote not as an end in itself—not as the panacea that would cure all the ills related to gender-based discrimination—but rather as an important weapon in the continuing fight for higher wages, better working conditions, and an end to the omnipresent menace of the lynch mob.

Today, as we reflect on the process of empowering Afro-American women, our most efficacious strategies remain those that are guided by the principle used by Black women in the club movement. We must strive to "lift as we climb." In other words, we must climb in such a way as to guarantee that all of our sisters, regardless of social class, and indeed all of our brothers, climb with us. This must be the essential dynamic of our quest for power—a principle that must not only determine our struggles as Afro-American women, but also govern all authentic struggles of dispossessed people. Indeed, the overall battle for equality can be profoundly enhanced by embracing this principle.

Afro-American women bring to the women's movement a strong tradition of struggle around issues that politically link women to the most crucial progressive causes. This is the meaning of the motto, "Lifting As We Climb." This approach reflects the often unarticulated interests and aspirations of masses of women of all racial backgrounds. Millions of women today are concerned about jobs, working conditions, higher wages, and racist violence. They are concerned about plant closures, homelessness, and repressive immigration legislation. Women are concerned about homophobia, ageism, and discrimination against the physically challenged. We are concerned about Nicaragua and South Africa. And we share our children's dream that tomorrow's world will be delivered from the threat of nuclear omnicide. These are some of the issues that should be integrated into the overall struggle for women's rights if there is to be a serious commitment to the empowerment of women who have been rendered historically invisible. These are some of the issues we should consider if we wish to lift as we climb.

During this decade we have witnessed an exciting resurgence of the women's movement. If the first wave of the women's movement began in the 1840's, and the second wave in the 1960's, then we are approaching the crest of a third wave in the final days of the 1980's. When the feminist historians of the twenty-first century attempt to recapitulate the third wave, will they ignore the momentous contributions of Afro-American women, who have been leaders and activists in movements often confined to women of color, but whose accomplishments have invariably advanced the cause of white women as well? Will the exclusionary policies of the mainstream women's movement—from its inception to the present—which have often compelled Afro-American women to conduct their struggle for equality outside the ranks of that movement, continue to result in the systematic omission of our names from the roster of prominent leaders and activists of the women's movement? Will there continue to be two distinct continuums of the women's movement, one visible and another invisible, one publicly acknowledged and another ignored except by the conscious progeny of the working-class women—Black, Latina, Native American, Asian, and white—who forged that hidden continuum? If this question is answered in the affirmative, it will mean that women's quest for equality will continue to be gravely deficient. The revolutionary potential of the women's movement still will not have been realized. The racist-inspired flaws of the first and second waves of the women's movement will have become the inherited flaws of the third wave.

How can we guarantee that this historical pattern is broken? As advocates and activists of women's rights in our time, we must begin to merge that double legacy in order to create a single continuum, one that solidly represents the aspirations of all women in our society. We must begin to create a revolutionary, multiracial women's movement that seriously addresses the main issues affecting poor and working-class women. In order to tap the potential for such a movement, we must further develop those sectors of the movement that are addressing seriously issues affecting poor and working-class women, such as jobs, pay equity, paid maternity leave, federally subsidized child care, protection from sterilization abuse, and subsidized abortions. Women of all racial and class backgrounds will greatly benefit from such an approach.

For decades, white women activists have repeated the complaint that women of color frequently fail to respond to their appeals. "We invited them to our meetings, but they didn't come." "We asked them to participate in our demonstration, but they didn't show." "They just don't seem to be interested in women's studies."

This process cannot be initiated merely by intensified efforts to attract Latina women or Afro-American women or Asian or Native American women into the existing organizational forms dominated by white women of the more privileged economic strata. The particular concerns of women of color must be included in the agenda.

An issue of special concern to Afro-American women is unemployment. Indeed, the most fundamental prerequisite for empowerment is the ability to earn an adequate living. At the height of its audacity, the Reagan government boasted that unemployment had leveled off, leaving only(!) 7.5 million people unemployed. These claims came during a period in which Black people in general were twice as likely to be unemployed as white people, and Black teenagers almost three times as likely to be unemployed as white teenagers.[5] We must remember that these figures do not include the millions who hold part-time jobs, although they want and need full-time employment. A disproportionate number of these underemployed individuals are women. Neither do the figures reflect those who, out of utter frustration, have ceased to search for employment, nor those whose unemployment insurance has run out, nor those who have never had a job. Women on welfare are also among those who are not counted as unemployed.

At the same time that the Reagan administration attempted to convey the impression that it had successfully slowed the rise of unemployment, the AFL-CIO estimated that 18 million people of working age were without jobs. These still-critical levels of unemployment, distorted and misrepresented by the Reagan administration, are fundamentally responsible for the impoverished status of Afro-American women, the most glaring evidence of which resides in the fact that women, together with their dependent children, constitute the fastest-growing sector of the 4 million homeless people in the United States. There can be no serious discussion of empowerment today if we do not embrace the plight of the homeless with an enthusiasm as passionate as that with which we embrace issues more immediately related to our own lives.

The United Nations declared 1987 to be the Year of Shelter for the Homeless. Although only the developing countries were the initial focus of this resolution, eventually it became clear that the United States is an "undeveloping country." Two-thirds of the 4 million homeless in this country are families, and 40 percent of them are Afro-American.[6] In some urban areas, as many as 70 percent of the homeless are Black. In New York City, for example, 60 percent of the homeless population are Black, 20 percent Latino, and 20 percent white.[7] Presently, under New York's Work Incentive Program, homeless women and men are employed to clean toilets, wash graffiti from subway trains, and clean parks at wages of sixty-two cents an hour, a mere fraction of the minimum wage.[8] In other words, the homeless are being compelled to provide slave labor for the government if they wish to receive assistance.

Black women scholars and professionals cannot afford to ignore the straits of our sisters who are acquainted with the immediacy of oppression in a way many of us are not. The process of empowerment cannot be simplistically defined in accordance with our own particular class interests. We must learn to lift as we climb.

If we are to elevate the status of our entire community as we scale the heights of empowerment, we must be willing to offer organized resistance to the proliferating manifestations of racist violence across the country. A virtual "race riot" took place on the campus of one of the most liberal educational institutions in this country not long ago. In the aftermath of the World Series, white students at the University of Massachusetts, Amherst, who were purportedly fans of the Boston Red Sox, vented their wrath on Black students, whom they perceived as a surrogate for the winning team, the New York Mets, because of the predominance of Black players on the Mets. When individuals in the crowd yelled "Black bitch" at a Black woman student, a Black man who hastened to defend her was seriously wounded and rushed unconscious to the hospital. Another one of the many dramatic instances of racist harassment to occur on college campuses during this period was the burning of a cross in front of the Black Students' Cultural Center at Purdue University.[9] In December 1986, Michael Griffith, a young Black man, lost his life in what amounted to a virtual lynching by a mob of White youths in the New York suburb of Howard Beach. Not far from Atlanta, civil rights marchers were attacked on Dr. Martin Luther King's birthday by a mob led by the Ku Klux Klan. An especially outrageous instance in which racist violence was officially condoned was the acquittal of Bernhard Goetz, who, on his own admission, attempted to kill four Black youths because he *felt* threatened by them on a New York subway.

Black women have organized before to oppose racist violence. In the nineteenth century the Black Women's Club Movement was born largely in response to the epidemic of lynching during that era. Leaders like Ida B. Wells and Mary

Church Terrell recognized that Black women could not move toward empowerment if they did not radically challenge the reign of lynch law in the land. Today, Afro-American women must actively take the lead in the movement against racist violence, as did our sister-ancestors almost a century ago. We must lift as we climb. As our ancestors organized for the passage of a federal antilynch law—and indeed involved themselves in the woman suffrage movement for the purpose of securing that legislation—we must today become activists in the effort to secure legislation declaring racism and anti-Semitism as crimes. Extensively as some instances of racist violence may be publicized at this time, many more racist-inspired crimes go unnoticed as a consequence of the failure of law enforcement to specifically classify them as such. A person scrawling swastikas or "KKK" on an apartment building may simply be charged—if criminal charges are brought at all—with defacing property or malicious mischief. Recently, a Ku Klux Klanner who burned a cross in front of a Black family's home was charged with "burning without a permit." We need federal and local laws against acts of racist and anti-Semitic violence. We must organize, lobby, march, and demonstrate in order to guarantee their passage.

As we organize, lobby, march, and demonstrate against racist violence, we who are women of color must be willing to appeal for multiracial unity in the spirit of our sister-ancestors. Like them, we must proclaim: We do not draw the color line. The only line we draw is one based on our political principles. We know that empowerment for the masses of women in our country will never be achieved as long as we do not succeed in pushing back the tide of racism. It is not a coincidence that sexist-inspired violence—in particular, terrorist attacks on abortion clinics—has reached a peak during the same period in which racist violence has proliferated dramatically. Violent attacks on women's reproductive rights are nourished by these explosions of racism. The vicious antilesbian and antigay attacks are a part of the same menacing process. The roots of sexism and homophobia are found in the same economic and political institutions that serve as the foundation of racism in this country and, more often than not, the same extremist circles that inflict violence on people of color are responsible for the eruptions of violence inspired by sexist and homophobic biases. Our political activism must clearly manifest our understanding of these connections.

We must always attempt to lift as we climb. Another urgent point on our political agenda—for Afro-American and for all progressive women—must be the repeal of the Simpson-Rodino Law. The Simpson-Rodino Law is a racist law that spells repression for vast numbers of women and men who are undocumented immigrants in this country. Camouflaged as an amnesty program, its eligibility restrictions are so numerous that hundreds of thousands of people stand to be prosecuted and deported under its provisions. Amnesty is provided in a restricted way only for those who came to this country before 1982. Thus, the vast numbers of Mexicans who have recently crossed the border in an attempt to flee intensified impoverishment bred by the unrestricted immigration of U.S. corporations into their countries are not eligible. Salvadorans and other Central Americans who have escaped political persecution in their respective countries over the last few years will not be offered amnesty. We must organize, lobby, march, and demonstrate for a repeal of the Simpson-Rodino Law.[10] We must lift as we climb.

When we as Afro-American women, when we as women of color, proceed to ascend toward empowerment, we lift up with us our brothers of color, our white sisters and brothers in the working class, and, indeed, all women who experience the effects of sexist oppression. Our activist agenda must encompass a wide range of demands. We must call for jobs and for the unionization of unorganized women workers, and, indeed, unions must be compelled to take on such issues as affirmative action, pay equity, sexual harassment on the job, and paid maternity leave for women. Because Black and Latina women are AIDS victims in disproportionately large numbers, we have a special interest in demanding emergency funding for AIDS research. We must oppose all instances of repressive mandatory AIDS testing and quarantining, as well as homophobic manipulations of the AIDS crisis. Effective strategies for the reduction of teenage pregnancy are needed, but we must beware of succumbing to propagandistic attempts to relegate to young single mothers the responsibility for our community's impoverishment.

In the aftermath of the Reagan era, it should be clear that there are forces in our society that reap enormous benefits from the persistent, deepening oppression of women. Members of the Reagan administration include advocates for the most racist, antiworking class, and sexist circles of contemporary monopoly capitalism. These corporations continue to prop up apartheid in South Africa and to profit from the spiraling arms race while they propose the most vulgar and irrational forms of anti-Sovietism—invoking, for example, the "evil empire" image popularized by Ronald Reagan—as justifications for their omnicidal ventures. If we are not afraid to adopt a revolutionary stance—if, indeed, we wish to be radical in our quest for change—then we must get to the root of our oppression. After all, *radical* simply means "grasping things at the root." Our agenda for women's empowerment must thus be unequivocal in our challenge to monopoly capitalism as a major obstacle to the achievement of equality.

I want to suggest, as I conclude, that we link our grass-roots organizing, our essential involvement in electoral politics, and our involvement as activists in mass struggles to the long-range goal of fundamentally transforming the socioeconomic conditions that generate and persistently nourish the various forms of oppression we suffer. Let us learn from the strategies of our sisters in South Africa and Nicaragua. As Afro-American women, as women of color in general, as progressive women of all racial backgrounds, let us join our sisters—and brothers—across the globe who are attempting to forge a new socialist order—an order which will reestablish socioeconomic priorities so that the quest for monetary profit will never be permitted to take precedence over the real interests of human beings. This is not to say that our problems will magically dissipate with the advent of socialism. Rather, such a social order should provide us with the real opportunity to further extend our struggles, with the assurance that one day we will be able to redefine the basic elements of our oppression as useless refuse of the past.

NOTES

1. Gerda Lerner, *Black Women in White America* (New York: Pantheon Books, 1972), p. 443.

2. These clubs proliferated the progressive political scene during this era. By 1916—twenty years later—50,000 women in 28 federations and over 1,000 clubs were members of the National Association of Colored Women's Clubs. See Paula Giddings's discussion of the origins and evolution of the Black Women's Club Movement in *When and Where I Enter* (New York: William Morrow, 1984), Chapters IV–VI.

3. Miriam Schneir, ed., *Feminism: The Essential Historical Writings* (New York: Vintage, 1972), pp. 138–142.

4. Ibid.

5. Children's Defense Fund, *Black and White Children in America: Key Facts* (Washington, D.C.: Author, 1985), pp. 21–22.

6. *WREE-VIEW*, Vol. 12, nos. 1 & 2, January–April, 1987.

7. Ibid.

8. Ibid.

9. The incidence of racial violence on college campuses has increased significantly since this speech was delivered in the summer of 1987. "Reports of racist acts at U.S. colleges and universities have been piling up at an increased pace for several years, and now, fresh incidents and controversies seem to arise almost daily" ("Racism, A Stain on Ivory Towers," *The Boston Sunday Globe*, 2/28/88, p. 1). In response to these incidents, students have organized themselves to improve the racial climate on their campuses. For example, in March 1988, a coalition of multiracial, domestic, and international students at Hampshire College in Amherst, Massachusetts, demonstrated the seriousness of their concerns by staging a building takeover and demanding specific correctives.

10. Unfortunately, the Simpson-Rodino bill was signed into law on November 6, 1987, with employer sanctions taking effect on June 1, 1988.

Facing Our
Common Foe: Women and
the Struggle Against Racism

At the time I accepted the invitation to participate in this conference, thousands of activists were feverishly working in the presidential-election campaign to defeat Ronald Reagan in his bid for a second term. For many of Reagan's opponents, the unthinkable occurred; preelection enthusiasm gave way to a sense of powerlessness and despair. Yet I want to suggest to you that no matter how dismal the state of affairs in our country may appear, we have not been absolutely vanquished. Contrary to popular belief, the 1984 elections did not express a consistent trend toward conservatism among the voting population. There was no sharp veering to the right in Congress, because—as paradoxical as it may seem—many who voted for Reagan also voted for Democratic congresspersons. This ambiguity in the electorate's decisions was further expressed by the fact that in some areas where Reagan received a majority of the vote,

—Address to a conference on "Women and the Struggle Against Racism" sponsored by the Minnesota Coalition for Battered Women, November 15, 1984.

progressive initiatives on employment and peace issues were passed.

What were the underlying dynamics of the election? Enormous numbers of people were lured into a trap, causing them to vote in diametrical opposition to their true interests. That Black people voted so unequivocally against President Reagan—more than 90 percent, in fact—indicates that, as a group, Afro-Americans are the least perplexed about the direction this country should be taking. Confusion did not reign in the Black community. There was no indecisiveness in the Rainbow Coalition about the issues we must raise: jobs, affirmative action, reduction of the military budget, and so on. The movement that crystallized around The Reverend Jesse Jackson's candidacy was also strategically the most advanced in the sense that it sought to forge a functional alliance embracing the struggles of the labor movement, Afro-American and other racially oppressed people, the women's movement, and the peace movement.[1]

It is too frequently assumed that white people are obligated to recognize Black people's leadership only when Afro-American equality is at issue—or that Chicanos, Puerto Ricans, Native Americans, and Asian-Pacific people are only qualified to speak on behalf of their own people and not on the conditions of society and humanity at large. It is imperative that those sectors of the women's movement that largely reflect the particular aspirations of their white middle-class constituencies challenge these erroneous assumptions. All too often—historically as well as at present—white leaders of the women's movement presume that when Black women raise our voices about the triple oppression we suffer, our message is at best of marginal relevance to their experiences. They have falsely presumed that women's issues can be articulated in isolation from issues associated with the Black movement and the labor movement. Their theories and practice have frequently implied that the purest and most direct challenge to sexism is one exorcised of elements related to racial and economic oppression—as if there were such a phenomenon as abstract womanhood abstractly suffering sexism and fighting back in an abstract historical context. In the final analysis, that state of abstraction turns out to be a very specific set of conditions: white middle-class women suffering and responding to the sexist attitudes and conduct of white middle-class men and calling for equality with those particular men. This approach leaves the existing socioeconomic system with its fundamental reliance on racism and class bias unchallenged.

It is possible for white women—especially those associated with the capitalist or middle classes—to achieve their own particular goals without securing any ostensible progress for their racially oppressed and working-class sisters. In response to the nomination of Geraldine Ferraro as the Democratic vice-presidential candidate, Reagan opportunistically boasted that the first woman president of this country would be a Republican, not a Democrat. Any feminist who welcomes this notion would be making a dreadful mistake. Let us not, after all, overlook the fact that the first woman Supreme Court justice, Reagan appointee Sandra Day O'Connor, has opposed women's right to abortion and has taken other distinctly antiwomen positions, as she has consistently placed herself on the conservative side of issues considered by the court.

It would not be inappropriate to raise questions concerning the underlying racism of some of Geraldine Ferraro's feminist supporters. Did they acknowledge, for example, that the mass movement galvanized by the 1984 Jesse Jackson candidacy played a pivotal role in the process by which a woman came to be included on a major presidential ticket for the first time in the history of this country? When Jesse Jackson revealed that, if he were selected as the Democratic presidential nominee, he would name a woman as his running mate, a serious and spirited discussion on women's political equality was initiated in national political circles. Why, then, was he virtually ignored by both the National Organization for Women and the National Women's Political Caucus? Why, when Mondale—who at the time had not even intimated that he was entertaining the idea of a woman running mate—was enthusiastically welcomed by these organizations, was Jesse Jackson not even invited to speak before their conventions? And after Mondale did indicate that he would consider a woman for that position, why did neither organization suggest that he interview a Black woman, along with the white women they proposed? This racist-inspired neglect on the part of these two leading women's organizations might have been less glaring were it not for the rich and abiding history of political leadership among Black women in this country. In recent times, Shirley Chisholm became the very first woman to announce her candidacy for the Democratic party's presidential nomination. That same year, in 1968, Charlene Mitchell, a Black woman from Harlem, was placed on the Communist Party's ticket as its presidential candidate, and sixteen years earlier, in 1952, a Black woman from Los Angeles by the name of Charlotta Bass was the Progressive party's vice-presidential candidate. In 1980 and 1984, I myself served as the vice-presidential candidate on the Communist Party ticket.

It is a well-known fact that for many years now, there

has been a tradition within the progressive community of placing women on the presidential ticket. Let us not forget that the Socialist party was the first political party to advocate woman suffrage. Furthermore, Black socialist W.E.B. DuBois, who eventually joined the Communist Party, was the most outspoken male advocate of women's rights to vote during the suffrage campaign that culminated in 1920.

In the wake of Geraldine Ferraro's selection as the Democratic vice-presidential nominee, buttons bearing the slogan, "Jesse Opened the Door, Ferraro Walked Through!" began to adorn the clothing of Rainbow Coalition activists, and were quite prominent at the Democratic Convention. But how many among Ferraro's feminist supporters acknowledged or even recognized the extent to which the daring militancy of the Jackson campaign facilitated Ferraro's ascension? There is a valuable lesson here: This is not the first time racism has obscured the part played by the Black liberation movement in promoting the democratic rights and liberties of the white majority—women as well as men. Unfortunately, far too few white feminists have delivered themselves from the influence of this dynamic.

Even as Black women welcomed the nomination of Geraldine Ferraro and grasped the momentous and historic nature of her candidacy, we did not uncritically assume that she would automatically represent the interests of all women. Rather, we recognized the urgent need for our own representative body, and before the conclusion of the Democratic Convention, Afro-American women announced the formation of a new organization, the National Political Congress of Black Women, under the leadership of Shirley

Chisholm. "Black women traditionally have always been involved in coalitions," Chisholm proclaimed.

> We've always found ourselves in a sense at the tail end. Neither the Black movement as such nor the women's movement as such in this country has addressed the political problems of blacks who are female.

How many white feminists, because they were so swept up in the euphoria occasioned by the first-time nomination of a woman vice-presidential candidate on a major-party ticket, failed to realize that their Black sisters had been excluded from this process? If it was necessary for Sojourner Truth to exclaim, "Ain't I a woman?" in 1851, Black women are still compelled to expose the invisibility to which we have been relegated, in both theory and practice, within large sectors of the established women's movement.

We are living in an era of profound global crisis for monopoly capitalism, a time of rising risks of nuclear omnicide, a time of threatened U.S. invasions of Central America, and a period in which the threat of fascism presents unprecedented dangers. The women's movement cannot afford to repeat its mistakes of the last century or even of the last decade. Errors and omissions—particularly those attributable to racism—must be immediately examined and measures taken to rectify them.

In the preelection discussion of the "gender gap," for example, the potential impact of race and class on women voters was not accorded the consideration it deserved. While it was predicted that 10–15 percent fewer women than men would vote for Ronald Reagan, in actuality there proved to be only a 4 percent differential: 61 percent of men and 57 percent of women voters chose Reagan for president of the United States. Observers of the 1984 elections assumed that women would vote against Reagan in such substantial numbers as a direct response to the serious deterioration of women's economic status during his first term. A June 1983 CBS/ *New York Times* poll revealed that only 39 percent of women, as compared to 60 percent of men, approved of Reagan's handling of the economy. This 21 percent "gender gap" was interpreted as a reflection of the process that has been referred to as the "feminization of poverty."

While the general rate of women's poverty is on the rise, it is not the case that all women have been equally affected by this process. Two out of every three poor adults are women, and one out of every five children is poor. Women head half of all poor families and more than half the children in female-headed households are poor. However, 68 percent of Black and Latino children in female-headed households are poor. Among Black women over sixty-five who live alone, the poverty rate is 82 percent. Yet despite the obvious fact that the burden of poverty is borne most distressingly by women of color, much of the public discussion regarding the "feminization of poverty" has concentrated on the "nouveau poor," that is, middle-class white women whose poverty is a function of marital separations and divorce. In typical racist fashion, the phenomenon of poverty was not recognized as a legitimate issue among women until it began to affect previously well-to-do white women. Yet Black women have been painfully familiar with the realities of economic privation since the days of slavery. Native American, Chicana, and Puerto Rican women likewise have always been poor in far greater numbers than their white sisters. The repercussions of the Reagan administration's economic policies on working people have been particularly devastating for women of color. The women who have learned most directly—and most profoundly—what it means to attempt to survive in a society that determines its priorities as a function of corporate profits are indeed Afro-American women and all their sisters of color.

The concept of the "feminization of poverty" must not be allowed to obscure the extent to which the entire Black community has suffered grave economic setbacks as a direct consequence of the domestic policies framed by the Reagan administration. The government's budget and tax policies have brought about a decline in income and in the standard of living for the average Black family in virtually every income stratum. In 1983, nearly 36 percent of all Black people lived in poverty—the highest percentage since the Census Bureau began collecting data on Black poverty in 1966. From 1980 to 1983, an additional 1.3 million Black people fell into the ranks of the officially poor. While white unemployment is lower now than at the beginning of Reagan's term of office—according to government statistics, that is—Black unemployment is now higher—16 percent, as compared to 14.4 percent when Reagan took office in 1981. The racial gap in unemployment has increased across the board—between black and white men, black and white women, and black and white youth.

George Gilder, one of the foremost philosophers of Reaganism, sophistically argues in his book *Wealth and Poverty* that Black women bear substantial responsibility for the impoverishment of the Black community. Challenging the notion that Black women are targets of double discrimination, he states that "[t]here is little evidence that black women suffer any discrimination at all, let alone in double doses."[2] Resurrecting the myth of the Black matriarchy, he suggests that Black women are intellectually and occupationally more advanced than their male counterparts. Moreover, he fallaciously reasons, their welfare benefits allow them special access to money—money that Black men do not have.

> Nothing is so destructive to . . . male values (such as male confidence and authority, which determine sexual potency and respect from the wife and children) as the growing, imperious recognition that when all is said and done, his wife can do better without him. The man has the gradually sinking feeling that his role as provider, the definitive male activity from the primal days of the hunt, through the industrial revolution and into modern life, has been largely seized from him, he has been cuckolded by the compassionate state.[3]

"In the welfare culture," Gilder more explicitly argues,

> money becomes not something earned by men through hard work, but a right conferred on women by the state. Protest and complaint replace diligence and discipline as the sources of pay. Boys grow up seeking support from women, while they find manhood in the macho circles of the street and the bar or in the irresponsible fathering of random progeny.[4]

Gilder contends that men who live with welfare mothers move from one woman to another and are both "beneficiaries and victims" of the welfare system. He suggests that hundreds of thousands of Black men do not marry and do not work because they are able to live off the benefits received by Black women, and that at the same time, the welfare system incites young Black women to become pregnant before they are in a position to raise a family.

> AFDC . . . offers a guaranteed income to any child-raising couple in America that is willing to break up, or to any teenaged girl over sixteen who is willing to bear an illegitimate child.[5]

If welfare benefits were anywhere as abundant as ideologues like Gilder make them out to be, acquiring the primary necessities of life for themselves and their children would not constitute such an arduous task for welfare mothers. Average AFDC benefits do not provide enough to raise a mother and her children above the poverty level, much less to support a man. Yet thanks to ideologues like Gilder, the myth persists that welfare mothers squander taxpayers' hard-earned money on Cadillacs and fur coats. Reagan himself has been known to fabricate stories about welfare fraud. "There's a woman in Chicago," he once said.

> She has eight names, thirty addresses, twelve social security cards. . . . She's got Medicaid, is getting food stamps, and she is collecting welfare under each of her names. Her tax-free cash income is $150,000.[6]

What Reagan was actually referring to was a case of welfare fraud in which a Chicago woman used *four* aliases, with which she managed to acquire about eight thousand dollars. Even though she did commit fraud, she nonetheless remained well below the income level required to lead a comfortable life in this country. Reagan concocted this lie for the purpose of publicly discrediting people—especially Black women—on welfare.

Media propagandists are now attributing a significant portion of the blame for poverty in the Black community to unmarried mothers—and particularly to teenagers who bear children. As James McGhee points out in the Urban League's 1984 *State of Black America* report:

> It is almost as if these observers propose that black families headed by females are subject to some inexorable law of nature that dictates that the heads of such families will be poor and their children disadvantaged, and that this same law does not apply to other blacks and other females.[7]

Media mystifications should not obfuscate a simple, perceivable fact: Black teenage girls do not create poverty by having children. Quite the contrary, they have babies at such a young age precisely because they are poor—because they do not have the opportunity to acquire an education, because meaningful, well-paying jobs and creative forms of recreation are not accessible to them. They have children at such a young age because safe, effective forms of contraception are not available to them.

Although 42 percent of Black families today are headed by women, it must not be assumed—as Gilder and others would have us believe—that virtually all Black single mothers receive welfare benefits. In 1980, two out of five Black single mothers were working. Since nearly a third of them worked on jobs subsidized by the federal government, Reagan's cutbacks in jobs programs—especially the Comprehensive Employment and Training Act (CETA) program—had a devastating effect on the employment of Black single mothers. According to the study conducted in connection with James McGhee's analysis, many unemployed single mothers in the Black community were not working because of health problems and because of the absence of child-care facilities. Hypertension affects 43 percent of Black single mothers, and 13 percent are stricken with diabetes.

In order for the women's movement to meet the challenges of our times, the special problems of racially oppressed women must be given strategic priority. During the early phases of the contemporary women's movement, women's liberationist issues were so narrowly construed that most white women did not grasp the importance of defending Black women from the material and ideological assaults emanating from the government. White women who were then primarily involved in the consciousness-raising process failed to comprehend the relationship between the welfare rights movement and the larger battle for women's emancipation. Neither did they understand the importance of challenging the propagandistic definition of Black women as "emasculating matriarchs" as a struggle in which all women who identified with women's liberation ought to have participated. Today, we can no longer afford to dismiss the racist influences that pervade the women's movement, nor can we continue to succumb to the belief that white women will be unable eternally to grasp the nature of the bonds that link them to their sisters of color.

It is no longer permissible for white women to justify their failure to struggle jointly with women of color by offering such frail excuses as, "We invited them to our meeting, but they just don't seem to be interested in women's issues." During the late 1960's and early 1970's, it was frequently suggested in women's liberation circles that Black,

Chicana, and Puerto Rican women were not interested in feminist issues because our awareness of male supremacy was not so advanced as that of the white women who hastened to participate in the antisexist consciousness-raising process. However, their articulation of the problem in these terms reflected their own particular class and racial backgrounds. Women of color—and white working-class women as well—suffered the effects of sexism in different ways than their sisters associated with the women's liberation movement and consequently felt that middle-class white women's issues were largely irrelevant to their own lives.

Economic issues certainly may not seem as central to white middle-class women as to women whose children may become irreparably malnourished if they are unable to find a job—or if they do not receive the welfare subsidies or food stamps so drastically reduced by the Reagan administration. The demand for jobs, the fight against plant shutdowns and against union-busting—these are women's struggles. While these struggles are waged by the labor movement as a whole, women have a special interest in them because we have been most severely hurt—particularly if we happen to be Black or Brown—by the Reagan administration's economic policies.

Students and professional women must learn to accept leadership from women who are actively involved in the labor movement. Women's groups not directly associated with the labor movement should, for example, seek to aid and support those women who are involved in strike activities. Consider the Chicana and Native American women who went out on strike, along with their brother miners, against Phelps Dodge in Morenci, Arizona. Alberta Chavez, who heads the women miners' and wives of miners' organization, had criminal charges imposed on her as she womaned a picketline in defiance of the police. Ms. Chavez appealed to women throughout the country for support.

In order to cultivate a strong women's presence in our movements against racism, women must resolutely defend affirmative action from such callous attacks as those mounted by the Reagan administration. Women and men of all racial and economic backgrounds should remember that the Black liberation movement formulated the strategy of affirmative action for the purpose of furthering the struggle against racism—and that this strategy was subsequently taken up by the women's movement as a means of facilitating the campaign against sexist discrimination. Affirmative action on the job as well as on the campus must not only be defended, but ultimately must be expanded so that it will assist all who currently suffer the discrimination wrought by our racist, sexist, capitalist society and government.

Women of color are particularly in need of an extensive, accessible child-care system. Such a system should be federally funded, nonracist, and nonsexist, and should be made available to all who need it. As we raise our demands for child care, we must simultaneously conduct an ongoing campaign against racism in the public-school system, insisting upon the implementation of bilingual public education on all levels.

We must not presume that authentic solidarity will automatically flow from the recognition of the simple fact that women of color are the most oppressed human beings in our society. Certainly, white women *should* feel compelled to lend their support to our struggles, but if they do not understand how their causes are substantially advanced by the victories won by women of color, they may inadvertently fall into ideological traps of racism even as they honestly attempt to challenge racist institutions. White women who labor under the illusion that only with their assistance will their "poor Black sisters" rise out of their deprivation—as if we need a Great White Sister Savior—have fallen prey to prevailing racist attitudes, and their activism could well prove more detrimental to our cause than beneficial. White women activists in the battered women's movement must especially beware of racist overtones in their conduct, of which they may be entirely unaware but to which women of color are highly sensitized. Lesbian organizations that are predominantly white should strive to understand the special impact of homophobia on women of color.

For the purpose of clarifying how middle-class white women benefit from the gains of their working-class sisters and sisters of color, try to visualize a simple pyramid, laterally divided according to the race and social class of different groups of women. White women are situated at the top—the bourgeoisie first, under which we place the middle classes and then white working-class women. Located at the very bottom are Black and other racially oppressed women, the vast majority of whom come from working-class backgrounds. Now, when those at the very apex of the pyramid achieve victories for themselves, in all likelihood the status of the other women remains unchanged. This dynamic has proven true in the cases of Sandra Day O'Connor and Jeane Kirkpatrick, who both achieved "firsts" as women in their respective fields. On the other hand, if those at the nadir of the pyramid win victories for themselves, it is virtually inevitable that their progress will push the entire structure upward. The forward movement of women of color almost always initiates progressive change for all women.

Working-class women, and women of color in particular, confront sexist oppression in a way that reflects the real and complex objective interconnections between economic, racial, and sexual oppression. Whereas a white middle-class woman's experience of sexism incorporates a relatively isolated form of this oppression, working-class women's experiences necessarily place sexism in its context of class exploitation—and Black women's experiences further contextualize gender oppression within the realities of racism.

Let us consider one of the most visible issues associated with the women's movement today within the framework of its relationship to the campaign against racism—the attempt to force women to surrender the right to control their bodies. Not only does the "pro-life" movement oppose the constitutional amendment that would guarantee women equal rights, they are pushing for a constitutional ban on abortions that, in effect, would extinguish women's most fundamental—and, ironically, most sacred—right: to determine what comes of and from their own bodies.

Terrorist tactics have been overtly encouraged and shamelessly implemented in the anti-abortion campaign of the so-called "right-to-lifers." During a peak year of the 1980s, there were some 147 incidents of violence and/or harassment—ranging from verbal abuse to the use of explosives to physically destroy the clinics—directed against abortion clinics and women seeking their services. In 1982, a group called the Army of God kidnapped the owner of a clinic in Illinois along with his wife. The two were held hostage for eight days, while their captors threatened to kill them if President Reagan did not announce an end to legal abortions.

Incidents such as these facilitated Reagan's manipulation of the abortion issue to encourage more widespread support of ultraright positions.

In considering the issue of abortion from a progressive vantage point, it is not enough to challenge the conservative factions that would deny women the right to control the biological processes of their bodies. It is also incumbent upon us to carefully examine the strategical and tactical approaches of the movement that strive to defend this basic right of all women. We must first ask why there have been so few women of color in the ranks of the abortion rights movement. And we must go on to consider a related issue: Why, with all the raging controversy surrounding women's right to abortion, has an equally burning question—that of women's right to be free of sterilization abuse—been virtually ignored? As a result of the 1977 Hyde Amendment, which withdrew federal funding for abortions, the likelihood that poor women will be forced to submit to sterilization surgery—knowingly or unknowingly—has increased, in spite of the fact that they may wish to remain capable of bearing children in the future. And how can we explain the fact that while there is presently no federal funding for abortions, over 90 percent of the cost of sterilization surgery is covered by the federal government? Sterilization abuse is sometimes blatant, but usually it occurs in more subtle ways, and its victims are most often Puerto Rican, Chicana, Native American, Black, and poor white women. One advocate of involuntary sterilization, the Nobel Prize-winning physicist William Shockley, has deemed 85 percent of Black Americans "genetically disadvantaged" and thus candidates for sterilization. Such policies must be challenged because we must protect not only women's right to limit the size of their families, but also their right to *expand* their families if and when they so desire.

This is only one example of the many ways in which we must formulate issues so as to ensure that they reflect the experiences of women of color. Certainly, there are many more issues related to the women's movement that, if explored, would demonstrate the extent to which racism often influences the way those issues are framed and publicly articulated. Such racist influences, as long as they pervade the women's movement, will continue to obstruct the building of multiracial organizations and coalitions. Thus, the *eradication* of those influences is a fundamental prerequisite to all endeavors undertaken by the women's movement. This process of exorcising racism from our ranks will determine whether the women's movement will ultimately have a part in bringing about radical changes in the socioeconomic structures of this country.

NOTES

1. Jackson's 1988 campaign realized the vision articulated in 1984, generating an impressive range of support extending from all sectors of the Black community to the labor movement and to progressive white individuals and organizations throughout the country. During the Democratic primaries, he received seven million votes, winning twelve hundred delegates, running a close second to Michael Dukakis. The Jackson campaign was indeed the centerpiece of the preconvention period. It demonstrated that a Black person can be taken seriously as a presidential candidate and that it is possible to forge the kind of coalition projected during the first campaign.

2. George Gilder. *Wealth and Poverty* (New York: Basic Books, 1981), p. 135.

3. Ibid., p. 115.

4. Ibid.

5. Ibid., p. 123.

6. *New York Times*, February 15, 1976.

7. James McGhee. "A Profile of the Black Single Female-Headed Household" in *The State of Black America, 1984* (New York: National Urban League, 1984), p. 43.

We Do Not Consent: Violence Against Women in a Racist Society

Even tonight and I need to take a walk and clear
my head about this poem about why I can't
go out without changing my clothes my shoes
my body posture my gender identity my age
my status as a woman alone in the evening/
alone on the streets/alone not being the point/
the point being that I can't do what I want
to do with my own body because I am the wrong
sex the wrong age the wrong skin and
suppose it was not here in the city but down on the beach/
or far into the woods and I wanted to go
there by myself thinking about God/or thinking
about children or thinking about the world/all of it
disclosed by the stars and the silence:
I could not go and I could not think and I could not
stay there

—Address presented at Florida State University, Talahassee, Florida, October 16, 1985. Originally published under the title "Violence Against Women and the Ongoing Challenge to Racism," Freedom Organizing Pamphlet Series, no. 5 (Latham, N.Y.: Kitchen Table/Women of Color Press, 1987).

alone
as I need to be
alone because I can't do what I want to with my own
body and
who in the hell set things up
like this
and in France they say if the guy penetrates
but does not ejaculate then he did not rape me
and if after stabbing him if after screams if
after begging the bastard and if even after smashing
a hammer to his head if even after that if he
and his buddies fuck me after that
then I consented and there was
no rape because finally you understand finally
they fucked me over because I was wrong I was
wrong again to be me being me where I was/wrong
to be who I am
which is exactly like South Africa
penetrating into Namibia penetrating into
Angola and does that mean I mean how do you know if
Pretoria ejaculates what will the evidence look like the
proof of the monster jackboot ejaculation on Blackland
and if
after Namibia and if after Angola and if after Zimbabwe
and if after all of my kinsmen and women resist even to
self-immolation of the villages and if after that
we lose nevertheless what will the big boys say will they
claim my consent:
Do You Follow Me: We are the wrong people of
the wrong skin on the wrong continent and what
in the hell is everybody being reasonable about . . .[1]

This excerpt from June Jordan's "Poem About My
Rights" graphically reveals the parallels between sexual vi-

olence against individual women and neocolonial violence against peoples and nations. Her message deserves serious consideration: We cannot grasp the true nature of sexual assault without situating it within its larger sociopolitical context. If we wish to comprehend the nature of sexual violence as it is experienced by women as individuals, we must be cognizant of its social mediations. These include the imperialist violence imposed on the people of Nicaragua, the violence of South African apartheid, and the racist-inspired violence inflicted on Afro-Americans and other racially oppressed people here in the United States.

Rape, sexual extortion, battering, spousal rape, sexual abuse of children, and incest are among the many forms of overt sexual violence suffered by millions of women in this country. When we are prohibited from exercising our abortion rights by the terroristic tactics of so-called "right-to-lifers" who bomb abortion clinics, and the criminal actions of the government as it withdraws federal subsidies for abortion, we experience violence aimed at our reproductive choices and our sexuality. Poor women, and specifically women of color, continue to fall prey to the surgical violence of sterilization abuse. Innumerable women unwittingly injure their bodies with the Dalkon Shield and other potentially fatal methods of birth control, while physically and mentally disabled women are presumptuously defined as nonsexual and therefore as requiring no special attention with respect to their birth-control needs. Reproductive rights, however, entail more than access to abortions and safe birth-control methods. They encompass, for example, the right of lesbians to have children outside of the confines of heterosexual relationships, and they will require nonrepressive laws governing new reproductive technologies involving donor insemination, in vitro fertilization, and surrogate motherhood.

These particular manifestations of violence against women are situated on a larger continuum of socially inflicted violence, which includes concerted, systematic violations of women's economic and political rights. As has been the case throughout history, these attacks most gravely affect women of color and their white working-class sisters. The dreadful rape epidemic of our times, which has become so widespread that one out of every three women in this country can expect to be raped at some point during her life, grimly mirrors the deteriorating economic and social status of women today. Indeed, as domestic racist violence mounts—and as global imperialist aggression becomes more widespread—so women can expect that individual men will be more prone to commit acts of sexual violence against the women around them. Though the Reagan administration attempts to displace the responsibility for this fact, it cannot escape blame for this rising threat of violence in our society. It is not only the most sexist government—the only one, for example, to actively oppose the Equal Rights Amendment at the same time that it supports the sexist and homophobic Family Life Amendment—and it is not only the most racist government, persistently seeking to dismantle thirty years of gains by the civil rights movement, but it is by far the most fiercely warmongering government of this century. Indeed, for the first time in the history of humankind, we face the very real threat of global nuclear omnicide.

Leaving aside this larger picture for the time being, let us focus more precisely on the recent history of our social consciousness regarding sexual violence against women.

When the contemporary antirape movement began to take shape during the early 1970's, shortly after the emergence of the women's liberation movement, the antirape movement—along with the campaign to decriminalize abortion—proved to be the most dramatic activist mass movement associated with the fight for women's equality. In January of 1971, the New York Radical Feminists organized a Rape Speak-Out, which, for the first time in history, provided large numbers of women with a forum from which to relate publicly their often terrifying individual experiences of rape.[2] Also in 1971, women in Berkeley, California, responded to the painfully discriminatory treatment received by rape survivors in police departments, hospitals, and courts by organizing a community-based twenty-four-hour crisis line known as Bay Area Women Against Rape. This crisis center became the model for countless similar institutions that arose throughout the country during the 1970's.

In 1971, Susan Griffin published a historic article in *Ramparts* magazine entitled "Rape: The All-American Crime." Her article opened with these words:

> I have never been free of the fear of rape. From a very early age I, like most women, have thought of rape as part of my natural environment—something to be feared and prayed against like fire or lightning. I never asked why men raped; I simply thought it one of the many mysteries of human nature.
>
> . . . At the age of eight . . . my grandmother took me to the back of the house where the men wouldn't hear, and told me that strange men wanted to do harm to little girls. I learned not to walk on dark streets, not to talk to strangers

or get into strange cars, to lock doors, and to be modest. She never explained why a man would want to harm a little girl, and I never asked.

If I thought for a while that my grandmother's fears were imaginary, the illusion was brief. That year, on the way home from school, a schoolmate a few years older than I tried to rape me. Later, in an obscure aisle of the local library (while I was reading *Freddy the Pig*), I turned to discover a man exposing himself. Then, the friendly man around the corner was arrested for child molesting.[3]

That virtually all of us can retrieve similar episodes from our childhood memories is proof of the extent to which misogynist violence conditions the female experience in societies such as ours. I recall that when I was an elementary-school student—I must have been about ten years old—a girlfriend of mine who lived around the corner suddenly disappeared for a week or so. During her absence from school, there were embarrassed whispers that she had been raped. When she returned, she never mentioned the reason for her absence, and no one dared attempt to break through her shroud of silence. I remember distinctly that all of the hushed conversations behind her back assumed that my friend had done something terribly wrong, and she walked around with a mysterious aura of immorality surrounding her for the rest of the time we spent in elementary school. More than any of the other girls, she was the target of the boys' sexual jeers. Assuming that she had transgressed the moral standards of our community, no one ventured to argue that she was the tragic victim of a crime that should never have gone uninvestigated or unpunished.

The antirape movement of the early seventies challenged

many of the prevalent myths regarding rape. For example, women militantly refuted the myth that the rape victim is morally responsible for the crime committed against her—a myth that is based on the notion that women have control over whether or not their bodies are violated during the act of rape. It used to be the case that defense attorneys would unhesitatingly presume to demonstrate the impossibility of rape by asking witnesses to insert a phallic object into a receptacle that was rapidly moved from one place to another. Oleta Abrams, one of the co-founders of Bay Area Women Against Rape, has related an anecdote that clearly reveals the most probable power relations in an actual rape incident. When a policeman asked a woman to insert his billy club into a cup that he continually maneuvered around, the woman simply took the club and struck him on the shoulder, causing him to drop the cup, into which she easily inserted the billy club.[4]

Another widespread myth is that if a woman does not resist, she is implicitly inviting the violation of her body. Transfer this assumption to the context of a case involving the criminal violation of property. Is a businessman asked to resist the encroachment of a robber in order to guarantee that his property rights will be protected by the courts? Even today, the persisting mystification of rape causes it to be perceived as a victim-precipitated crime, as was the case in the ruling of a Wisconsin judge who, in 1977, found a fifteen-year-old male's rape of a teenager who was wearing a loose shirt, Levi's, and tennis shoes to be a "normal" reaction to the "provocative" dress of the young woman.

Although there is a pervasive fear among most women of being raped, at the same time, many women feel that it cannot really happen to them. Yet *one* out of *three* women will be sexually assaulted in her lifetime, and *one* out of *four* girls will be raped before she reaches the age of eighteen. Despite these startling statistics, there is only a 4 percent conviction rate of rapists—and these convictions reflect only the minute percentage of rapes that are actually reported.

Rape happens anytime, anywhere, to females of all ages. Infants of four months have been raped, and women over ninety years old have been raped, although the single largest group of rape survivors is composed of adolescent girls between the ages of sixteen and eighteen. Rape happens to women of all races and all classes, regardless of their sexual orientation.

Although most of us tend to visualize rape episodes as sudden, unanticipated attacks by perverse strangers, most victims actually know their rapists and, in fact, more than half of all rapes occur in the home of either the survivor or the offender. Furthermore, it is often assumed that rape is an act of lust and that, consequently, rapists are simply men who cannot control their sexual urges. The truth is that most rapists do not impulsively rape in order to satisfy an uncontrollable sexual passion. Instead, men's motives for rape often arise from their socially imposed need to exercise power and control over women through the use of violence. Most rapists are not psychopaths, as we are led to believe by typical media portrayals of men who commit crimes of sexual violence. On the contrary, the overwhelming majority would be considered "normal" according to prevailing social standards of male normality.

Certainly the most insidious myth about rape is that it is most likely to be committed by a Black man. As a direct consequence of the persistent insinuation of racism into prevailing social attitudes, white women are socialized to harbor far more fear that they will be raped by a Black man than by a white man. In actuality, however, for the simple reason that white men compose a larger proportion of the population, many more rapes are committed by white men than by Black men. But as a consequence of this country's history of ubiquitous racism in law enforcement, there are a disproportionately large number of Black men in prison on rape convictions. The myth of the Black rapist renders people oblivious to the realities of rape and to the fact, for example, that over 90 percent of all rapes are intraracial rather than interracial. Moreover, as has been pointed out in studies on sexual assault—and as indeed was the case during the era of slavery—proportionately more white men rape Black women than Black men rape white women. Nonetheless, the average white woman in this country maintains a far greater suspicion of Black men than of white men as potential rapists. These distorted social attitudes, which are racist by their very nature, constitute an enormous obstacle to the development of a movement capable of winning substantive victories in the struggle against rape.

If we examine the reasons why laying the foundation for an effective multiracial antirape movement has been such an arduous process, we discover that the confounding influence of the myth of the Black rapist looms large. During the early 1970's, when the antirape campaign was in its infancy, the presence of Afro-American women in that movement was a rarity. This no doubt was in part attributable to the underdeveloped awareness regarding the interconnectedness of racism and sexism in general among the white women who pioneered the women's liberation movement. At the same time, antirape activists failed to develop an understanding of the degree to which rape and the racist use of the fraudulent rape charge are historically inseparable. If, throughout our history in this country, the rape of Black women by white men has constituted a political weapon of terror, then the flip side of the coin has been the frame-up rape charge directed at Black men. Thousands of terroristic lynchings have been justified by conjuring up the myth of the Black rapist.

Since much of the early activism against rape was focused on delivering rapists into the hands of the judicial system, Afro-American women were understandably reluctant to become involved with a movement that might well lead to further repressive assaults on their families and their communities. Yet, at the same time, Black women were and continue to be sorely in need of an antirape movement, since we comprise a disproportionately large number of rape survivors. It is all the more ironic that Black women were absent from the contemporary antirape movement during its early days, since antirape activism actually has a long history in the Black community. Probably the first progressive movement to launch a frontal challenge to sexual violence was the Black Women's Club Movement, which originated in the late 1890's based on the antilynching activities of women like Ida B. Wells.[5] Today, organizations such as the National Black Women's Health Project in Atlanta are conducting organizing and educational campaigns around such issues as rape and sterilization abuse.

Certainly any woman can understand the intense anger that characterized the first phase of the antirape campaign. Throughout all of history, the judicial system and society in general had not even acknowledged women as legitimate victims of a crime if the crime committed against them was rape. Much of women's cumulative rage about rape was understandably aimed at men. When a feminist theoretical foundation for the campaign began to develop, the theories tended to bolster and legitimize indiscriminate antimale anger by defining rape as an inevitable product of masculine nature. Masculinity was understood not so much in terms of its social determinations, especially under conditions of capitalism, but rather as an immutable biologically and psychologically determined product of men's inherent nature.

These theories most often did not take into account the class and racial components of many rapes suffered by working-class white women and women of color. In fact, the failure of the antirape movement of the early 1970's to develop an analysis of rape that acknowledged the social conditions that foster sexual violence as well as the centrality of racism in determining those social conditions, resulted in the initial reluctance of Black, Latina, and Native American women to involve themselves in that movement. Throughout Afro-American women's economic history in this country, for example, sexual abuse has been perceived as an occupational hazard. In slavery, Black women's bodies were considered to be accessible at all times to the slavemaster as well as to his surrogates. In "freedom," the jobs most frequently open to Black women were as domestic workers. This relegation of Black women to menial jobs did not begin to change until the late 1950's, and there is ample documentation that as maids and washerwomen, Black women have been repeatedly the victims of sexual assault committed by the white men in the families for which they worked.

Sexual harassment and sexual extortion are still occupational hazards for working women of *all* racial backgrounds. In a survey conducted by *Redbook*, in 1976, 90 percent of the nine thousand respondents reported that they had encountered sexual harassment on the job.[6] According to Julia Schwendinger, in her book entitled *Rape and Inequality*, one congresswoman discovered that a certain congressman was asking prospective women employees whether they engaged in oral sex, as though this were a requirement for the job.[7]

If we assume that rape is simply a by-product of maleness, a result of men's anatomical construction or of an immutable male psychological constitution, then how do we explain the fact that the countries that are now experiencing an epidemic of rape are precisely those advanced capitalist countries that face severe economic and social crises and are saturated with violence on all levels? Do men rape because they are men, or are they socialized by their own economic, social, and political oppression—as well as by the overall level of social violence in the country in which they live— to inflict sexual violence on women?

Sexual violence often flows directly from official policy. In Vietnam, as Arlene Eisen has pointed out in her book *Women in Vietnam*, U.S. soldiers often received instructions for their search and destroy missions that involved "searching" Vietnamese women's vaginas with their penises.[8] The following observation has been made about sexual violence under the conditions of fascist dictatorship in Chile:

> The tortures of women included the agony of scorching their nipples and genitals, the blind terror of applying shock treatments to all parts of their bodies, and, of course, gang rape. An unknown number of women have been raped; some of them pregnant after rape have been refused abortions. Women have had insects forced up their vaginas; pregnant

women have been beaten with rifle butts until they have aborted.[9]

Indeed, rape is frequently a component of the torture inflicted on women political prisoners by fascist governments and counterrevolutionary forces. In the history of our own country, the Ku Klux Klan and other racist groups have used rape as a weapon of political terror.

Rape bears a direct relationship to all of the existing power structures in a given society. This relationship is not a simple, mechanical one, but rather involves complex structures reflecting the interconnectedness of the race, gender, and class oppression that characterize the society. If we do not comprehend the nature of sexual violence as it is mediated by racial, class, and governmental violence and power, we cannot hope to develop strategies that will allow us eventually to purge our society of oppressive misogynist violence.

In our attempt to understand the structure of rape, it would be a grievous mistake to limit our analysis to individual cases or even to conduct our analysis only in terms of male psychology. The only logical strategies for the elimination of rape that would follow from this type of analysis would be a reliance on repression to punish and deter rapists. But as the use of the repressive paraphernalia of the state has generally demonstrated, further crimes are seldom deterred by punishment meted out to those who have been caught committing them. Thus, for each punished rapist, how many more would be lurking in our neighborhoods—indeed, in our workplaces and even in our homes? This is not to argue that men who commit rape should go unpunished, but rather that punishment alone will not stem the rising tide of sexual violence in our country.

The experience of the 1970's demonstrates that antirape strategies that depend primarily on law-enforcement agencies will continue to alienate many women of color. Indeed, the experience of Black women has been that the very same white policemen who are charged with protecting them from rapists and other criminals will sometimes go so far as to rape Black women in their custody. Ann Braden, a veteran civil rights organizer, has referred to such conduct by southern white policemen who arrested Black women activists during the civil rights struggle and subsequently raped them. I recall an experience I had as a graduate student in San Diego when a friend and I found a young Black woman, beaten and bloody, on the shoulder of the freeway. She had been raped by several white men and dropped by the side of the road. When the police found her, they, too, raped her and left her on the freeway, barely conscious. Because these cases are by no means isolated, Black women have found it extremely difficult to accept policemen as enforcers of antirape measures.

Moreover, police forces often employ tactics ostensibly designed to capture rapists, but whose ulterior aim is to augment their arsenal of racist repression. During the 1970's, a rapist was terrorizing the Berkeley community. He initially attacked scores and scores of Black women. Hundreds of rapes in the area were attributed to "Stinky," as he was called. However, it was not until he began to rape white women, and specifically when he raped a well-known Black woman television newscaster, that the police began to turn their attention to the case. They released a description of him so general that it probably fit no less than a third of the Black men in the area, and countless men were arrested for no other reason than that they were Black. Moreover, Berkeley police proposed to the city council a strategy to capture Stinky that involved hiring more police officers, acquiring helicopters and other aircraft, and using tracking and attack dogs. The police department had been attempting to get approval for the use of dogs since the student movement of the 1960's, but had failed because of community opposition. In order to implement their repressive agenda, they seized a moment in which many of the women in the community felt utterly terror-stricken. Unfortunately, the antirape movement, which at that time was almost exclusively white, did not perceive the hidden agenda of the police force and agreed to cooperate with the proposed strategy. Thus, they unwittingly became collaborators in a plan that would inevitably result in increased police brutality in Berkeley's Black community.

The antirape movement today must remain cognizant of such potential pitfalls. It must beware of concentrating exclusively on strategies such as crisis centers, which, important as they may be, treat only the effects and leave the cause of the crime unremedied. The very same social conditions that spawn racist violence—the same social conditions that encourage attacks on workers, and the political posture that justifies U.S. intervention in Central America and aid to the apartheid government in South Africa—encourage sexual violence. Thus, sexual violence can never be completely eradicated until we have successfully effected a whole range of radical social transformations in our country.

We must strive to link our efforts to ensure the safety of women with our concern for the safety of this planet. It is no coincidence that the explosion of sexual violence in this country takes place at a time when the United States government has developed the means with which to annihilate human life itself. It is no accident that a government that spends $41 million an hour on the most devastating instruments of violence ever known in human history, also encourages the perpetuation of violence on all levels of society, including sexual attacks on women. It has been calculated that $200 million, just five hours of military spending, could provide annual support for sixteen hundred rape crisis centers and battered women's shelters.

We will never get past the first step in eliminating the horrendous violence done to women in our society if we do not recognize that rape is only one element in the complex structure of women's oppression. And the systematic oppression of women in our society cannot be accurately evaluated except as it is connected to racism and class exploitation at home and imperialist aggression and the potential nuclear holocaust that menace the entire globe.

The antirape movement should therefore attempt to establish closer ties to other campaigns for women's rights, as well as to labor struggles wherever they unfold. If we are militant activists challenging violence against women, we must also fulfill our duties as fearless fighters against police violence, and we must express our passionate solidarity with the racially and nationally oppressed people who are its main targets. We must defend, for example, the memory of Eleanor Bumpurs, the sixty-seven-year-old Black woman from the Bronx who was murdered in 1984 by New York Housing Authority policemen because she took a stand and attempted to resist eviction.

The banners and voices we raise against rape must also be raised against racist and anti-Semitic Ku Klux Klan and

Nazi violence. They must be raised in defense of political prisoners like Leonard Peltier, the Native American Indian leader, and Johnny Imani Harris, the Black prison activist who, after twelve long years, has just recently been removed from Alabama's death row.

If we aspire to eradicate sexual violence, we must also call for the immediate freedom of Nelson and Winnie Mandela and all political prisoners in South Africa. Our sisters and brothers in Nicaragua and El Salvador need our solidarity, as do our Palestinian friends who are fighting for their land and their dignity. And certainly, we cannot forget our Iranian sisters who are attempting to complete the democratic revolution that has been violently stifled by Khomeini's Islamic Republic.

To recognize the larger sociopolitical context of the contemporary epidemic of sexist violence does not, however, mean that we ignore the specific and concrete necessity for the ongoing campaign against rape. This battle must be waged quite concretely on all of its myriad fronts. As we further shape the theoretical foundation of the antirape movement and as we implement practical tasks, let us constantly remind ourselves that even as individual victories are claimed, the complete elimination of sexist violence will ultimately depend on our ability to forge a new and revolutionary global order, in which every form of oppression and violence against humankind is obliterated.

NOTES

1. June Jordan, *Passion* (Boston: Beacon Press, 1980).
2. cf Noreen Connell and Cassandra Wilson, ed., *Rape: The First*

Sourcebook for Women by New York Radical Feminists (New York: New American Library, 1974).

3. Jo Freeman, ed., *Women: A Feminist Perspective*, 1st ed. (Palo Alto: Mayfield Publishing Co., 1975).

4. Julia and Herman Schwendinger, *Rape and Inequality* (Beverly Hills: Sage Library of Social Research, 1983), p. 23.

5. cf Paula Giddings, *When and Where I Enter* (New York: William Morrow, 1984), Chapter 6.

6. Schwendinger, op. cit., p. 50.

7. Ibid.

8. Arlene Eisen, *Women in Vietnam* (San Francisco: People's Press, 1975), p. 62.

9. Schwindinger, op. cit., p. 203.

Sick and Tired of Being
Sick and Tired: The Politics
of Black Women's Health

Politics do not stand in polar opposition to our lives. Whether we desire it or not, they permeate our existence, insinuating themselves into the most private spaces of our lives. As a starting point for this discussion of the politics of Black women's health, I propose that we consider the lived experience of one courageous individual who, as she poignantly documents her own personal-health battles, harvests lessons that elucidate our collective quest for wellness. "How do I provide myself," Audre Lorde asks,

> . . . with the best physical and psychic nourishment to repair past, and minimize future damage to my body? How do I give voice to my quests so that other women can take what they need from my experiences? How do my experiences with cancer fit into the larger tapestry of my work as a Black

—Address given at Bennett College, Greensboro, North Carolina, August 29, 1987, before a conference organized by the North Carolina Black Women's Health Project. Originally published under the title "The Politics of Black Women's Health," in *Vital Signs* 5, no. 1, February 1988.

woman, into the history of all women? And most of all, how do I fight the despair born of fear and anger and powerlessness which is my greatest internal enemy?

I have found that battling despair does not mean closing my eyes to the enormity of the tasks of effecting change, nor ignoring the strength and the barbarity of the forces aligned against us. It means teaching, surviving and fighting with the most important resource I have, myself, and taking joy in that battle. It means, for me, recognizing the enemy outside and the enemy within, and knowing that my work is part of a continuum of women's work, of reclaiming this earth and our power, and knowing that this work did not begin with my birth nor will it end with my death. And it means knowing that within this continuum, my life and my love and my work has particular power and meaning relative to others.

It means trout fishing on the Missisquoi River at dawn and tasting the green silence, and knowing that this beauty too is mine forever.[1]

On this continuum of women's work, upon which Audre Lorde situates herself and her precious offerings, the pursuit of health in body, mind, and spirit weaves in and out of every major struggle women have ever waged in our quest for social, economic, and political emancipation. During the past decade, we have been the fortunate beneficiaries of the valuable work of health activists like Byllye Avery and Lillie Allen of the National Black Women's Health Project, who have perceptively and passionately addressed Black women's health issues and have begun to chart out paths toward wellness in all its myriad forms. The Project has chosen as its motto Fannie Lou Hamer's well-known lament: we are sick and tired of being sick and tired.

We have become cognizant of the urgency of contextualizing Black women's health in relation to the prevailing political conditions. While our health is undeniably assaulted by natural forces frequently beyond our control, all too often the enemies of our physical and emotional well-being are social and political. That is why we must strive to understand the complex politics of Black women's health.

One would assume that the U.S. Constitution, which guarantees to all individuals "life, liberty and the pursuit of happiness," by implication assures that all citizens of this country are entitled to be healthy. However, it is not really necessary to derive this right from the Constitution, for health ought to be universally recognized as a basic human right. Yet in this society, dominated as it is by the profit-seeking ventures of monopoly corporations, health has been callously transformed into a commodity—a commodity that those with means are able to afford, but that is too often entirely beyond the reach of others. Pregnant Black women, uninsured and without the means to pay hospital entrance fees, have been known to give birth in parking lots outside the hospitals that have refused them entrance. In other instances, poor Black women who are subscribers to health plans have been denied treatment because hospital officials have presumptuously argued that they were lying about their insurance coverage.

Sharon Ford, a young Black woman on welfare in the San Francisco Bay Area, gave birth to a stillborn child because two hospitals declined to treat her, even though she was covered by a health plan. Aware of a serious problem with her pregnancy, Ms. Ford sought treatment at the hospital nearest her home. When she informed officials there that she was covered by a certain medical plan, she was sent by them to the hospital associated with that plan, despite the fact that her critical condition obviously warranted emergency intervention. Officials at the second hospital, who claimed that their computerized list of subscribers to that plan did not include her name, instructed her to go to yet another facility, known as the poor people's medical warehouse in that area. In the meantime, however, three hours had passed, and by the time she was treated by doctors at the third hospital, her unborn baby had died. Ironically, it was later discovered that the insurance company had been tardy in delivering the subscriber list that, indeed, contained Sharon Ford's name. While this is the tragic story of a single Black woman, it cannot be dismissed as an aberration. Rather, it is symptomatic of dangerous trends within the health-care industry.

Because so many programs designed to ameliorate the conditions of poor people—inadequate as they may have been—have been abolished or cut back in recent years, accessibility to health services has become an especially pressing problem. The major barrier to Black women's health is poverty—and during the Reagan years, our communities became increasingly impoverished. The number of poor people increased by more than 6 million, and according to the Physicians' Task Force on Hunger, as many as 20 million people in this country suffered from want of food. A dire consequence of poverty is malnutrition and a plethora of diseases emanating from the lack of adequate sustenance. Malnutrition, which can cause maternal anemia and toxemia, a potentially fatal condition for a pregnant woman, is also implicated in premature births and infant death.

Associated with higher rates of chronic illnesses such as heart disease, arthritis, and diabetes, poverty causes its victims to be more susceptible to hypertension and lung, stomach, and esophageal cancer. The National Black Women's Health Project has pointed out that while proportionately fewer Black women than white women suffer from breast cancer, more Black women are likely to die from it. Furthermore, as cervical cancer rates have decreased among white women, they have risen among Black women. For reasons that require no explanation, poverty increases vulnerability to mental illness. Of all groups in this country, Black women have the highest rates of admission to outpatient psychiatric services. It has been argued by health activists that most adult Black women live in a state of psychological stress.

Two out of three poor adults are women, and 80 percent of the poor in the United States are women and children. This means that women are the majority of recipients of many health and nutritional programs sponsored by the federal government. Because Black women are disproportionately represented among the beneficiaries of these social services, they have been hurt most deeply by the cutbacks in the federal budget. When the cutbacks in Aid to Families with Dependent Children occurred, most of the women who lost AFDC also lost their Medicaid coverage. Federal cuts in the Maternal and Child Health Block Grant resulted, in almost all states, in the reduction of services offered in maternal and child health clinics, or in the curtailment of the number of people eligible to receive this care. As a consequence, almost a million people, most of whom are children and women of childbearing age, became ineligible to receive services at community health centers. This means, for example, that fewer Black women now receive prenatal care, a fact that has fatal implications, because babies born to mothers receiving no prenatal care are three times more likely to die in infancy than those whose mothers do receive such care. At the same time, federal funding for abortions has become virtually nonexistent, while the government continues to strongly subsidize surgical sterilization. This process is a vicious cycle, further entrenching poor people in conditions that make ill health inevitable. Standing at the intersection of racism, sexism, and economic injustice, Black women have been compelled to bear the brunt of this complex oppressive process.

Afro-American women are twice as likely as white women to die of hypertensive cardiovascular disease, and they have three times the rate of high blood pressure. Black infant mortality is twice that of whites, and maternal mortality is three times as high. Lupus is three times more common among Black women than white, thus the funds channeled into research to discover a cure for it have been extremely sparse. Black women die far more often than white women from diabetes and cancer.

This cycle of oppression is largely responsible for the fact that far too many Black women resort to drugs as a means—however ineffective it ultimately proves to be—of softening the blows of poverty. Because of intravenous drug use in the Black community, a disproportionately large number of Black women have been infected with AIDS. Although the popular belief is that AIDS is a disease of gay white men, the truth is that Afro-Americans and Latinos are far more likely to contract AIDS than whites. This is true among gays, among IV drug users, among heterosexual partners, and among children. Black and Latino men are 2.5 times as likely to get AIDS as white men. Latina women are nine times as likely as white women to contract AIDS. But the most frightening statistic is reserved for Black women, who are twelve times more likely to contract the AIDS virus than white women.

Four times as many black women as white women die of homicide. In the meantime, under the Reagan administration, hospitals serving predominantly poor Black communities—including those with excellent trauma units, designed to treat victims of violence—were closed down. Such was the case with Homer G. Phillips Hospital in St. Louis, the largest teaching hospital for Black medical students in the country. On average in this country, there is one doctor per fifteen hundred people, but in Central Harlem, there is only one doctor per forty-five hundred people.

A statement by the Public Health Association of New York City during the first year of the Reagan administration warned:

> The health of the people of New York City is actively endangered by the already imposed cuts and by the threatened cuts in funding for health care services and for medical care services. To express ourselves in clear language, so there is no misunderstanding: We are talking about dead babies whose deaths can be prevented; we are talking about sick children and adults whose illnesses can be prevented; we are talking about misery for older people whose misery can be prevented. We are speaking of these unspeakable things in a wealthy country and in a wealthy state, whose people deserve better. The malignant neglect of federal, state and local governments is literally killing people now and will kill, and destroy the lives of, many more in the future. We urge a massive infusion of federal and state funds to restore and

> rebuild services now, before the consequences of their break-
> down demonstrate in even more tragic and dramatic ways
> the human and economic cost of this neglect.[2]

Outside South Africa, the United States is the only major
industrial country in the world that lacks a uniform national
health-insurance plan. While this country is sorely in need
of a national health-care plan, there has been an increasing
trend toward the privatization of health care. As one author
plainly put it, the principle of the Reagan administration
was "Profits Before People, Greed Before Need, and Wealth
Before Health."[3]

In urging the privatization of health care, the government
has prioritized the profit-seeking interests of monopoly corporations, leaving the health needs of poor people—and
especially poor Black women—to be callously juggled
around and, when need be, ignored. For-profit hospitals
often refuse outright to treat poor, uninsured patients, and
they engage in the unethical practice of "dumping" welfare
recipients on public hospitals, even when those patients are
in urgent need of treatment. This was the unfortunate fate
of Sharon Ford, whose baby became one of the many fa-
talities of a process that places profits before people's health
needs.

Because the hospital emergency room is a major setting
for medical treatment in the Black community, this pattern
of the privatization of hospitals is having an especially devastating impact on Black people—and on Black women in
particular. In 1983, only 44.1 percent of Afro-Americans
receiving health care made visits to a private doctor in her
or his office. On the other hand, 26.5 percent went to a
hospital emergency room and 9.7 percent received treatment

in an outpatient clinic. By contrast, 57 percent of white patients receiving medical care visited private physicians, 13 percent went to emergency rooms and 16 percent went to outpatient clinics.

The degree to which private corporations threaten to monopolize health-care services is revealed by the fact that the Hospital Corporation of America, which controlled only two hospitals in 1968, now controls almost five hundred and is a dominant force in the hospital business. Other such corporations are Cigna, American Medical International, and Humana. Health-care workers—a majority of whom are women in the lower-paying occupations—have also suffered from this privatization trend, for corporate takeovers of public hospitals have frequently resulted in union-busting and a subsequent freeze on wages and cutbacks on benefits.

> The only ones who benefit from a competition system of medical care are the rich, who will have to pay less for health care for the poor, and those providers who skim the cream off the medical market and leave the real problems to a diminished and even-more-inadequately-financed public sector. It is yet another example of the basic Reagan policy of serving the rich, encased in a Trojan Horse, this one labeled "cost containment," "deregulation," and "free choice."[4]

It is clearly in the interests of Afro-American women to demand a federally subsidized, uniform national health-insurance plan. We need subsidized programs that reflect the progressive experiences of the women's health movement over the last decade and a half, programs that emphasize prevention, self-help, and empowerment.

One of the main obstacles to the development of a national

health plan is the same unrelenting pressure placed by government on all social programs benefiting poor people, and people of color in particular—namely, the runaway military budget. Since 1980, the military budget has more than doubled, taking approximately $100 billion from social programs that were underfunded to begin with. Between 1981 and 1986, $1.5 trillion was spent on military programs. The *Women's Budget*, published by the Women's International League for Peace and Freedom, points out:

> Defense Department spending in 1986 was $292 billion, but the actual costs of the military in that year were over $400 billion if hidden costs like veterans' benefits, nuclear warheads in the Department of Energy's budget, and the part of the interest on the national debt attributable to past military expenditures are taken into account.[5]

The budget cuts that have affected health and other social services are not, strictly speaking, cuts, but rather transfers of funds from the civilian to the military budget. Instead of providing poor people with adequate food stamps, the corporations that make up the military-industrial complex are awarded gigantic defense contracts. Ironically, forty-five of the top one hundred defense contractors who received more than $100 billion in prime-contract awards in 1985 later came under criminal investigation.[6]

As we examine the political forces responsible for the violation of Black women's health rights, it becomes clear that the increasing militarization of our economy is culpable in a major way. The politics of Black women's health are also directly influenced by the general assault on democracy in this country, which reached a high point during the Reagan years. It is not a coincidence that a government that would sabotage the rights of every citizen of this country by permitting the development of a secret junta controlled by the Central Intelligence Agency and the National Security Council also seriously infringed upon the health rights of Black women and all poor people.

The Iran-contra Hearings revealed the extent to which we were rapidly heading in the direction of a police state. The CIA operatives involved used government and private funds to support the most reactionary forces in the world— from the contras in Nicaragua to the South African–supported UNITA in Angola. They were involved in gun running, drug trafficking, bombings, assassinations, and attempted overthrows of democratically elected governments.

The executive branch of the government during the Reagan years was dominated by corporate executives and by top military men. They continued to serve the monopoly corporations as they carried out the bellicose policies of the military. As they conducted undeclared wars in various parts of the world, they were responsible for a domestic war against poor people, one of whose battlefronts involved the cutbacks in health services whose effects have been so detrimental to Black women.

Reagan's 1987 nomination of the ultraconservative Robert Bork to the Supreme Court was yet another offensive against the welfare of Black women and others who suffer from racism, sexism, and economic exploitation. As Senator Edward Kennedy so poignantly observed, "Robert Bork's America is a land in which women would be forced into back-alley abortions, Blacks would sit down at segregated lunch counters, [and] rogue police would break down citizens' doors in midnight raids . . ." Fortunately, progressive forces joined hands and succeeded in blocking the confirmation of Judge Bork to the Supreme Court.

It is from the success of progressive campaigns such as this one, as well as from the important work of organizations such as the National Black Women's Health Project, that all of us who are concerned with remedying the deplorable state of health care in this country must glean important lessons. We must learn consistently to place our battle for universally accessible health care in its larger social and political context. We must recognize the importance of raising our voices in opposition to such backward forces as Robert Bork and the outdated conservatism he represents. We must involve ourselves in the anti-apartheid movement in solidarity with our sisters and brothers in South Africa, who not only suffer the ill effects of negligent health care but are daily murdered in cold blood by the South African government. We must actively oppose our government's continuing bid for Congressional support of contra aid; we must not allow our sisters and brothers in Nicaragua, whose revolutionary strivings have made health care available to all of their country's inhabitants on an equal basis, to be defeated.

While we fight for these larger victories, we must also learn to applaud the small victories we win. As I opened with the wise words of Audre Lorde, so I would like to conclude with this passage taken from her book *A Burst of Light*:

> Battling racism and battling heterosexism and battling apartheid share the same urgency inside me as battling cancer. None of these struggles is ever easy, and even the smallest

victory must be applauded, because it is so easy not to battle at all, to just accept, and to call that acceptance inevitable.[7]

NOTES

1. Audre Lorde, *The Cancer Journals* (San Francisco: Spinsters Ink, 1980), p. 17.

2. Alan Gartner, Colin Greer, and Frank Riessman, *What Reagan Is Doing to Us* (New York: Harper and Row, 1982), p. 50.

3. Ibid., p. 48.

4. Ibid., p. 46.

5. "The Women's Budget," Women's International League For Peace And Freedom, 1986, p. 3.

6. Ibid.

7. Audre Lorde, *A Burst of Light* (Ithaca, N.Y.: Firebrand Books, 1988), pp. 116–17.

Peace Is a Sisters' Issue Too: Afro-American Women and the Campaign Against Nuclear Arms

As Black women, we have ever so many reasons to celebrate the strong tradition of activism forged by our foremothers over the course of many generations of struggle. Since its founding in 1975, the Los Angeles Black Women's Forum has reinforced and contemporized this tradition. In the same way that our great grandmothers relied on the luminous leadership of women like Ida B. Wells and Mary Church Terrell, who attempted to eradicate the terror of lynching during the first part of this century, today we look to the president of this organization, Maxine Waters, who relentlessly challenges the present-day lynchers, exploiters, and militarists.

In 1985, I was privileged to hear Maxine Waters present the keynote address at an affair organized by the National Political Congress of Black Women. Reminding us of the painful reality that only one Black woman then served in Congress, she passionately urged us to begin working for

—Address to the Black Women's Forum, Los Angeles, November 16, 1985.

the election of at least three more Black women to Congress in 1986—Cardiss Collins, the incumbent from Illinois, Kay Hall from Indiana, and Jan Douglass from Georgia. Although I wholeheartedly agreed with her, I could not help but speculate that if Maxine Waters herself were elected to Congress, Ronald Reagan and his cohorts would find it all the more difficult to execute their heinous schemes. She is without doubt one of the great political figures of our times; she does not embrace politics as a means of advancing her own career, but rather as a forum for the fearless defense of all who suffer the pervasive injustices of our society. Maxine Waters is our gift as Afro-American women to those who dream of extricating themselves from oppression in this country and throughout the world. But it is not enough simply to be proud that we have such a woman pleading our cause as an assemblywoman in Sacramento and as a nationally acclaimed political leader. We must be willing to support her as she takes her stand. We must stand with her as she confronts the racists, the male supremacists, the accomplices of apartheid, the union-busters, and the militarists who currently run our country.

The 1980's have been marked by an alarming erosion of the civil rights victories that were the culmination of decades of extraordinary struggles and enormous human sacrifices. While some of us may feel we have reached the mountaintop and are living the dream envisioned by Martin Luther King, Jr., most members of our community are suffering more intensely today than ever before. Our jobs are rapidly slipping away from us as plants shut down and as key areas of the economy become robotized and militarized. We continue to be overrepresented in low-paying occupations and underrepresented in high-paying occupations. We are unemployed, we are in prison, we are on death row, we are victims of a horrendous rise in police crimes, our rights to education have dangerously deteriorated, our access to health care is near extinction, our ability to wield the ballot—especially in the deep South—faces the looming threat of increased restriction: In a flagrant reversal of our hard-won suffrage victories, grass-roots voting-rights activists in the Black Belt counties of Alabama have been arrested by the federal government on trumped-up charges of voter fraud. This is an egregious assault on the legacy of Dr. Martin Luther King, Jr., and on all who stood with him on the battleground for civil rights.

These are times of great suffering for Black people. When we consider that the assaults on the rights and lives of Afro-Americans have been menacingly complemented by the proliferation of sexist discrimination and by concerted attacks on workers of all races and nationalities, we find that we are not alone in our experience of social affliction. We furthermore share with every human being on this planet the historically unprecedented peril of nuclear omnicide. As Black people, as women, as Black women, we need to develop a more serious appreciation of the peace movement and the hope it alone is capable of generating for the future of our children. It is imperative that we reevaluate our failure to participate in the peace movement in numbers that are commensurate with our peace sentiments, and that we hasten to rectify this situation.

We can no longer afford to assume that peace is a white folks' issue. How can we in good conscience separate ourselves from the fight for peace when nuclear bombs do not know how to engage in racial discrimination? And if it were at all conceivable that nuclear fallout could be programmed to kill some of us while sparing others, I can guarantee you that the warmakers in this country would see to it that Black people would be its first victims. What would be accomplished by victory in our struggles against racism, what purpose would be served by assisting our sisters and brothers in South Africa to overthrow Botha's apartheid regime, when, in the final analysis, we might all be annihilated in a nuclear conflagration? Peace, my sisters and brothers, is a Black folks' issue and it is a Black women's issue. The failure to realize this might very well cost us our lives.

Our history as Afro-Americans should render us especially sensitive to peace issues, for since the days of the African slave trade, we have been subjected to warlike aggression by a white ruling class in its quest for profit and power. More than anyone else, we should also understand that peace is not an abstract state of affairs, but rather is inextricably connected with our ability to achieve racial, sexual, and economic justice. When we speak of peace, we must also speak of freedom.

Black people yearned for peace during World War II, but we also knew that peace would not be achieved without the defeat of German fascism and Japanese militarism. Moreover, we recognized then that authentic peace ought to have included the defeat of racism at home as well. In 1934, a Black woman sharecropper from Alabama by the name of Capitola Tasker attended an international women's conference in Paris that militantly opposed German fascism and warned against the impending threat of war. This Black woman went to Paris to register her people's passionate opposition to Hitler, but she also resonantly proclaimed that the peoples of the world should be made aware of the fascistlike terror being visited upon Black people in the United

States. She described the lynchings and mob murders in the South and persuasively compared them to the threat of Nazi terror in Europe. Today, my sisters and brothers, we should be following her example by exposing the connections between the threat to world peace posed by the Pentagon and the escalating domestic attacks on the lives of our people.

If it is true, as Dr. Martin Luther King, Jr., once said, that "a nation that continues year after year to spend more money on military defense than on programs of social uplift is approaching spiritual death," then our country has spiritually died many times over since the advent of the Reagan administration. In cities like Chicago, Black youngsters suffer from diseases of malnutrition that afflict children in the famine areas of Africa, yet school breakfast and lunch programs have been abolished in order to provide the weapons developers and manufacturers with an unending supply of money.

And who are the financial supporters of the Pentagon? Not the huge corporations that are offered exorbitant military contracts. As a matter of fact, some of the country's largest military contractors pay absolutely no federal income tax—Lockheed, General Electric, Boeing, and General Dynamics paid no taxes between 1981 and 1983, even though they had combined profits totaling $10 billion. Some of these companies even managed to get money back from the government. In other words, you and I support the Pentagon. Over sixty cents of each income-tax dollar goes to the Pentagon. A person who earns twenty-two thousand dollars a year will have given over an entire year's salary to the Pentagon between 1985 and 1989, all for the production of more MX missiles, more Trident and Cruise missiles, and for the further research and development of the Strategic Defense Initiative, popularly known as Star Wars.

As the economy becomes increasingly militarized, jobs are devoured. The escalating militarization of the economy is one of the major causes of unemployment, and of the scandalous levels of joblessness for Black people. Statistics from the Bureau of Labor indicate that $1 billion spent on weapons produces twenty-one thousand military jobs, but that the same $1 billion would produce an average of twenty-five thousand nonmilitary jobs and as many as fifty-four thousand jobs in hospitals and seventy-two thousand jobs in educational services. Black people, and Black women in particular, who seek work in large numbers in the fields of health and education, are especially hurt by the pattern of militarization of the economy. Considering that billions of dollars are transferred from the civilian to the military sector and that only 1 percent of all employed women work under military contracts or in the armed services, we can begin to comprehend the devastating impact of militarization on our economic security as Black women.

The Women's International League for Peace and Freedom has pointed to some of the concrete implications of the distorted priorities of our government. The production and deployment of fifty-seven MX missiles, for example, costs $7 billion. If we were to take that money and transfer it to human services, we could restore the cuts and indeed expand funding for Aid to Families with Dependent Children (AFDC). With the $1 billion required to reactivate two World War II battleships, we could provide emergency help for the homeless. With another $1 billion channeled into the production of four hundred M-1 tanks, the cost of prescription medication for 7.5 million senior citizens could be subsidized. And with $500 million, which represents only one B-1 bomber out of a planned one hundred, immunizations and basic health supplies for 50 million children in Asia, Africa, and Latin America could be provided.

Interestingly, the media have attributed the recent disarmament proposals on the part of the Soviet Union to its need to decrease military production in order to provide more goods and services for its population, allegedly suffering the effects of an ailing economy. Well, if anyone's economy is ailing, it is ours. If any government needs to decrease military spending in order to minister to the needs of its people, it is the U.S. government. What is wrong with the Soviet Union wanting to cut back on military production in order to build more housing, provide more health care, subsidize more education for its people? That is the only rational thing to do.

Many of us are associated with the mass challenge to apartheid. Yet we tend to forget that South Africa is a developing nuclear power. Moreover, if a nuclear war does occur, it will in all likelihood be occasioned by a conflict over a situation not unlike those presently existing in South Africa, Central America, and the Middle East.

In recent years, some Black people have indicated that they are tired of demonstrating and that mass street marches are passé. But, sisters, we cannot afford to tire of demonstrating, and mass marches will not become obsolete until we have achieved equality, justice, and peace. We must make ourselves heard, and we must put forth our demands as vigorously and resolutely as we can. Peace is a sisters' issue too.

Slaying the Dream:
The Black Family and
the Crisis of Capitalism

(with Fania Davis)

> God knows there was plenty wrong with Walter Younger—
> hard-headed, mean, kind of wild with women—plenty
> wrong with him. But he sure loved his children. Always
> wanted them to have something—be something. Big Walter
> used to say, he'd get right wet in the eyes sometimes, lean
> his head back with the water standing in his eyes and say,
> "Seem like God didn't see fit to give the black man nothing
> but dreams—but He did give us children to make them
> dreams seem worthwhile."
>
> —Lorraine Hansberry, *Raisin in the Sun*[1]

Within every culture in the world, children represent
promises of material and spiritual riches that their mothers
and fathers have been unable to attain. African-American
culture is no exception, and, as Lorraine Hansberry's character insists, children make more realizable those grand as-

—Earlier versions of this article, under the title "The Black Family and the
Crisis of Capitalism," appeared in *Black Liberation Journal* 9, no. 1, Spring 1986,
and in *Black Scholar* 17, no. 5, September/October 1986.

pirations toward progress that are not within their parents' reach. In the often-quoted words of José Martí, "Children are the hope of the world."

Throughout the centuries following the forcible transplantion of African people from their motherland to America, children have represented the very special promise of freedom for an entire people. Even as Black people's efforts to hold on to and strengthen their family ties were cruelly assaulted, the family has remained an important cauldron of resistance, forging and preserving a vital legacy of collective struggle for freedom. Though our great-grandmothers and great-grandfathers may not have expected to free themselves from slavery or sharecropping or Mr. Charlie's kitchen, they could at least pass on their dream of freedom to successive generations.

Today, however, the lives and futures of those to whom the dream should be offered are in great jeopardy. According to the most recent report of the Children's Defense Fund, Black children today are far more likely to be born into devastating conditions of poverty than they were five years ago. They are twice as likely as white children to die in the first year of their lives, and they are three times as likely as whites to be misplaced in classes for the educable mentally retarded. Afro-American children are twice as likely as white children to have no parent employed, to be unemployed as teenagers, and to live in substandard housing. They are three times as likely as whites to have their mothers die in childbirth. Moreover, those between the ages of fifteen and nineteen are four times as likely as white children to be incarcerated in jails and prisons.[2] Perhaps the most startling reality about the present predicament of Black children is that in some major urban centers they have been found to suffer from kwashkiorkor and marasmus, diseases of malnutrition commonly found in famine areas of Africa.

Our families, of course, have never corresponded in structure and function to the prevailing social ideal. First of all, original African cultural traditions had a much broader definition of the family than that which prevails in this society; it was not limited merely to biological parents and their progeny. Especially during the earlier phases of the African presence in the Americas, the extended family was a vital tradition. Second, the brutal economic and political pressures connected with slavery and continuing throughout subsequent historical eras have consistently prevented African-American family patterns from conforming to the dominant family models. Finally, Black people, both during and after the slave era, have been compelled to build, creatively and often improvisationally, a family life consistent with the dictates of survival. Yet because the Afro-American family does not reflect the norm, it has been repeatedly defined as pathological in character and has been unjustly blamed for the complex problems that exist within the Black community—problems often directly attributable to the social, economic, and political promotion of racism. This is not, of course, to deny that Black families are beset with serious difficulties. But to focus myopically on family problems as the basis for the oppression of the Afro-American community—as if setting the family in order will automatically eradicate poverty—is to espouse the fallacious "blame the victim" argument.

The current ideological blame-shifting, which targets the Black family, reflects the broader trend of placing the family in general—falsely represented as an isolated, privatized area of social life—at the heart of dangerous dysfunctions that affect the moral well-being of U.S. society. As the traditional male-supremacist hierarchy in the family, based on male "providers" and their economically dependent wives and children, is being fundamentally challenged by the increasing participation of working-class women in the labor force, ultraconservative advocates argue that the family itself is falling apart due to, among other things, the rising support of abortion rights and socialized child care. They even go so far as to claim that homosexuality threatens to destroy the fabric of the family. In this way, they attempt to divert public attention from some of the most serious demands of the contemporary women's movement: equal pay for jobs of comparable worth, reproductive rights, paid maternity leave, and subsidized child care—demands that are increasingly antimonopoly in character.

The era ushered in by the election of Ronald Reagan to the presidency has been marked by a renewed propagandistic attempt to deem the breakdown of the Black family structure responsible for the erosion of material well-being in the Black community. It is frequently pointed out that almost half of all Afro-American families revolve around single women and that 55 percent of Black babies are born to unmarried mothers—a substantial number of whom are under the age of twenty.

The Reagan administration audaciously purported that the welfare system brought about this breakdown in the structure of the Black family. Thus, the logical solution would involve the reduction of government programs and the requirement that individuals on welfare offer their labor to the state, as well as the implementation of programs designed to apprehend absent fathers, compelling them to contribute to the support of their children.

A conservative economist argues that the welfare system encourages female dependence on government handouts and diverts male attention away from the pursuit of legitimate work:

> In the welfare culture money becomes not something earned by men through hard work, but a right conferred on women by the state. Protest and complaint replace diligence and discipline as the sources of pay. Boys grow up seeking support from women, while they find manhood in the macho circles of the street and the bar or in the irresponsible fathering of random progeny.[3]

Moreover, Gilder maintains, AFDC

> offers a guaranteed income to any child-raising couple in America that is willing to break up, or to any teenaged girl over sixteen who is willing to bear an illegitimate child.[4]

Robert B. Carleson, Reagan's adviser for social policy development, put forth similar arguments, holding existing government social programs responsible for the increasing number of single-parent, female-centered households. Moreover, he asserted that the main problem is the failure in the Black community to form families at all. The implication, of course, is that the Black community is morally out of sync with the rest of U.S. society. Yet statistical evidence demonstrates that the great majority of female-centered households are caused not by unwed women, but by the breakup of married couples with children. Of the single women heading families, only one-fourth have never been married: 28.7 percent are married with an absent spouse, 22.2 percent are widowed and 21.9 percent are divorced.[5] Would the withdrawal of welfare payments resurrect dead fathers, annul divorces, or cause unemployed husbands to return to their wives and children? Would it make sex education available to teenagers and bring into being safe, effective, and accessible contraceptive measures? This last question has serious implications, since the birthrate among single Black teenagers actually declined during the 1970's—a fact that clearly flies in the face of the prevailing belief that Black teenage girls are having more babies than ever before. What has caused a disproportionate number of births to unmarried teenagers is the even more rapid decline in the birthrate among older and married Black women.[6] These groups are far more likely to rely on contraception and to have abortions—and, indeed, to become sterilized—than unmarried Black teenagers.

While the relatively high rates of pregnancy among Black teenagers are certainly cause for alarm, it should not be assumed that the isolated eradication of this problem would automatically lead to a significant reduction of the impoverishment of the Black population, as James McGhee has pointed out in his article on the Black family in the Urban League's 1985 *The State of Black America* report:

> There is nothing inherent in the married state that leads to higher family income. Black married couples have higher incomes primarily for two reasons: because both householders are often in the labor force and because males generally have higher median incomes than females do.[7]

The impoverishment of Black families will not miraculously disappear as a consequence of reducing the high rate of teenage pregnancy to a more manageable level. However urgent a problem this may be, it is by no means the root cause of the Black community's deteriorating economic status. On the contrary, it is a symptom of a deeply rooted structural crisis in the U.S. monopoly-capitalist economy— the reverberations of which are being felt most acutely in the Afro-American community. There is a direct correlation between the unprecedented rates of unemployment among Black teenagers and the rise in the birthrate among Black women under twenty. Yet the Reagan administration's policy shapers consistently formulated the problem of teenage pregnancies in terms that implicitly held Black girls partially responsible for the depressed state of the Black community.

Conservative theorists who express outrage about the accelerated rate of Black teenage pregnancy and the corresponding breakdown of the Black family rely, directly or by implication, upon old historical distortions about Black women's—and men's—morality, or alleged lack thereof. They accuse government welfare programs of promoting the ethical failures of the Black community. Shortly after the Black Family Summit that took place in the spring of 1984, William F. Buckley, Jr., praised the Black organizations—the NAACP, the Urban League, and others—that had finally recognized that the Black family's problems were the Black community's problems. In an article appearing in the *National Review*, Buckley quoted John Jacob, president of the National Urban League, who claims that ". . . we may have allowed our just anger at what America has done to obscure our own need for self-discipline and strengthened community values." At the same time, Buckley criticized the Black Family Summit for not recognizing that there is an "inverse correlation between state welfare and black progress."

> Welfare checks do more than merely convert a government voucher into food and rent. They tend to affect the spirit and particularly they tend to dissolve the natural bonds of loyalty a man feels toward the woman he has impregnated and the child born of a union that is increasingly fleeting rather than lasting.[8]

There are many destructive pressures exerted on Black families, such as the decreasing availability of quality education to young Black people, the proliferation of drugs and the prevalence of other antisocial phenomena that are directly encouraged by the racist institutions of this country. The most devastating encumbrance, though, especially among young Black men and women, is pervasive joblessness. Current observations on the Black family continually point out that between 1960 and 1980, the percentage of single Black women with children rose from about 21 percent to 47 percent. What is seldom noted, however, is that during the same historical period, the percentage of employed adult Black men plummeted from approximately 75 percent to 55 percent. It is common knowledge that government census figures undercount the Black population, which means that probably fewer than half of Afro-American males in this country actually hold jobs. Official unemployment rates among Black teenagers project a 50 percent rate of joblessness, but the reality is that fewer than 20 percent actually hold jobs. The rest are simply not counted as being a part of the labor force. Moreover, to unemployment must be added the more subtle symptoms of underemployment and undercompensation. According to the Children's Defense Fund annual report, if almost half of all Black children are poor (as compared to one in six white children) it is because the median income of Black families is less than 60 percent that of white families. In 1983, half of all Black families had incomes below fourteen thousand dollars.[9]

While the difficulties besetting the family should by no means be dismissed, any strategies intended to alleviate the prevailing problems among poor Black people that methodologically target the family for change and leave the socioeconomic conditions perpetuating Black unemployment and poverty intact are doomed to failure from the outset. In 1965, Daniel Moynihan authored the government report entitled *The Negro Family: Case for National Action*. The document had important strategic implications, for it attempted to justify the withdrawal of government measures that had been specifically designed to counter the racist edge of the social crisis that seemed destined to hurl the Black community into the throes of permanent impoverishment. The real problem, Mr. Moynihan argued, was the matriarchal structure of the Black family. As far as government programs were concerned, those that directly intervened in Black family life were deemed most desirable. Once the Black family began to reflect the prevailing nuclear (male-supremacist) model, problems such as unemployment and the decline in the quality of housing, education, and health care, would eventually be solved.

During the Reagan administration, official spokesmen proposed the curtailment of government programs designed to bring some relief to poor families—ostensibly in order to revive a two-parent family structure in the Black community. Just as the ulterior aim of the Moynihan Report was to provide a philosophical justification for reversing government policy meant to eradicate the causes of racism in U.S. society, the Reaganite strategy was designed to deny the existence of institutionalized forms of racism in the post-civil rights era. Reagan propagandists asserted that Black people are suffering in the 1980's because of our own inadequacies, and that we must deal with our problems without the assistance of such institutions as the AFDC welfare program.

While the 1984 Black Family Summit did not entirely dismiss the deleterious impact of objective economic factors on the Black community, it placed the greatest emphasis on strategies of volunteerism. John Jacobs of the Urban League asserted that it is high time Black people begin independently to address our problems. "In concentrating on the wrongs of discrimination and poverty," he said, "we have neglected the fact that there is a lot we can do about our problems ourselves."[10] Even as most conference participants assented in principle to the notion that help from the government is essential, the need for self-help was the clear conclusion of the gathering. This is the consensus that emerged from the two hundred delegates present:

> Black churches could create credit unions, establish and support Black entrepreneurship, use their publishing houses to publish Black authors and teach sex education. Affluent Blacks could make venture capital available to Black businesses. Organizations could register voters and urge them to vote in elections from the school board to the Presidency. Youths could consider the military for employment and skills training.[11]

In a 1985 *New York Times* article entitled "Restoring the Traditional Black Family," Eleanor Holmes Norton set forth views on the Black family that reveal the influence of blame-the-victim syndrome. Though she acknowledges the destructive pressures of extreme poverty and unemployment, she also argues that the causes for the actual disruption of our families must be sought elsewhere. "If economic and social hardships could in themselves destroy family life, the family could not have survived as the basic human unit throughout the world," she theorizes.[12] According to Norton, the true culprit today is the "destructive ethos" and the "self-perpetuating culture of the ghetto." Moreover, she argues,

> [t]he remedy is not as simple as providing necessities and opportunities. The family's return to its historic strength will require the overthrow of the complicated predatory ghetto subculture, a fact demanding not only new government approaches, but active Black leadership and community participation and commitment.[13]

Unfortunately, Norton succeeds in contemporizing and exacerbating the approach launched by Moynihan in the 1960's. Norton urges the government to replicate existing successful training and jobs programs for "ghetto males." She further calls for the systematic duplication of "successful workfare programs such as those in Baltimore and San Diego," and suggests that public assistance programs should "concentrate on changing lifestyles as well as imparting skills and education." She emphasizes the need for "ghetto institutions" and Black middle-class individuals with "ghetto roots" to engage in a range of self-help remedies, including family planning, counseling, sex education, day care and, most important, passing on the enduring Black American values of "hard work, education, respect for the Black family and, notwithstanding the denial of personal opportunity, achieving a better life for one's children." Although Norton makes obligatory mention of the fact that "[t]he disruption of the Black family today is, in exaggerated microcosm, a reflection of what has happened to American family life in general,"[14] her proposed solutions focus myopically on what she calls "the ghetto." Dr. Martin Luther King's critique of the original Moynihan Report, in which he called attention to the danger that "problems will be attributed to innate Negro weaknesses and used to justify neglect and rationalize oppression," is no less relevant to Norton's formulations of 1985.[15]

In the meantime, Moynihan has reassessed his views. He now argues that precisely because of the pervasiveness of single-parent families and the impoverishment of those families, the resulting problems should be attributed not simply to Black people, but to society as a whole. And while this modified description of the problem certainly represents an improvement, Moynihan still admits that he is incapable of proposing anything other than piecemeal solutions. He cautions that "[w]e do not know the processes of social change well enough so as to be able confidently to affect them,"[16] and merely suggests that personal tax exemption and welfare payments be increased to take inflation into account and that the government assume responsibility for enforcing laws against drug trafficking.

In an attempt to address specific problems associated with the Black family crisis, organizations such as the National Council of Negro Women have developed practical com-

munity programs. According to Dorothy Height, president
of the council, SMART (Single Mothers Advance Rapidly
through Training)

> . . . is a program designed to improve the employability
> skills of young mothers through classroom and on-the-job
> training. The ultimate goal is to help stabilize the life of the
> young mother and to help her see the need for education,
> training and marketable and life skills development.
> Our first goal must be to prevent the initial pregnancy.
> The second goal must be to ensure that a girl who has had
> a baby does not have a second. Then, we must make sure
> that pregnant teen mothers receive adequate prenatal care so
> that prematurity, low birth weight and birth defects do not
> additionally handicap their babies' lives. Our efforts must be
> targeted and tailored to reach all young people.[17]

However, if such goals are to be achieved, employment
and educational opportunities must be readily available. And
the fact is that the U.S. economy has been rapidly phasing
out jobs traditionally held by Black people, thus shoving
ever-larger numbers of our people to the outer margins of
this country's economic life. The severe structural problems
that can be detected within the Black family are symptomatic of a much larger problem: the structure of the economic system is on the verge of collapse. Eleanor Holmes
Norton placed "permanent generational joblessness," with
roots in the post–World War II era, "at the core of the
meaning of the American ghetto," but she simply proposed
that we need to "cull the successful aspects" from existing
training and jobs programs and duplicate these models nationwide.[18] The discordance between the magnitude of the

assessed problem and the triviality of the proposed solution is, to say the least, deeply disturbing.

The era in which we live has seen the entrance of the world capitalist economy into a phase of decline. Any strategy that does not acknowledge this fundamental reality and fails to appreciate the new level of the capitalist crisis will result in temporary and superficial treatment of its symptoms and will only allow it to continue on its current path. Furthermore, a faulty assessment of the problem will lead to a dangerous underestimation of the bold and radical stands that must be taken if we are to eradicate such capitalist phenomena as unemployment and homelessness. Steel and other basic industries have sharply declined, leaving Black people especially vulnerable to unemployment. Entire plants have been shut down or transferred to other parts of the country or abroad. Between 1979 and 1984, 11.5 million jobs were permanently lost due to cutbacks in production. Other features of the structural crisis include compounding of huge budget deficits, the unprecedented scope of inflation, the agricultural crisis, and the urban crisis.

The increasing militarization of the economy is perhaps the most prominent feature of the structural crisis of capitalism. The retooling of the productive process in accordance with the dictates of the military-industrial complex creates the means with which to produce untold billions of dollars in weapons whose destructive potential is unprecedented. In the process, however, Black people are literally robbed of jobs—at the rate of thirteen hundred jobs for each increase of $1 billion in the military budget.[19] The runaway U.S. military budget is at the heart of an economic "tangle of pathology"—to borrow Moynihan's terminology—which is currently causing the devastation of the Black community and the resulting structural problems within the Black family. Since 1980, the military budget has literally doubled, while nonmilitary programs have been slashed by almost $100 billion. Between 1981 and 1985, military budgets have totaled $1.2 trillion, and the Pentagon has proposed $2 trillion more for the next five years. To place this amount in perspective, let us consider that $3 million spent every day for the past two thousand years would equal $2 trillion—the amount the Pentagon proposes to spend in the next five years. In 1986, the Pentagon spent nearly $1 billion a day, which amounts to $41 million an hour, or $700,000 a minute.[20]

While health programs are being steadily cut to feed the Pentagon's exorbitant military budget, fewer than half of all preschool Black children are being immunized against polio, diphtheria, tetanus, and smallpox. The Reagan administration convinced Congress to make cuts in student financial assistance programs at a time when almost half of all Black seventeen-year-olds are functionally illiterate. The nation's welfare recipients, 53 percent of whom are Black, receive an average of only $111 a month each—and only a little more than half the nation's poor children are being reached by the AFDC programs. Yet Reagan attacked the program, and his policies were responsible for severe cuts, which began in 1980. Following Reagan's entrance into the White House, 6 million more people fell into the ranks of the poor. Twenty million were hungry, yet 1 million were completely taken off the food-stamp rolls. While subsidized housing was cut by 63 percent, homelessness continued to grow at an alarming rate. These are but a few examples of the consequences of an increasingly militarized economy.

Given the historic decline and contraction of the contemporary capitalist economy, exacerbated in large part by the rapid militarization of the productive process, it is plain that conditions of mass unemployment and rising poverty in our communities will persist unless a radical antimonopoly program of jobs with peace is instituted. The Income and Jobs Action Act of 1985, introduced by Representatives Charles Hayes (D-Ill.) and John Conyers (D-Mi.) incorporates a strategy to end unemployment which will be of inestimable value in future efforts to combat joblessness, both within the context of a progressive congressional agenda and in mass movements for full employment. Hayes and Conyers call for a federal jobs program at decent wages that will bring full employment with affirmative action; a thirty-five-hour work week with no cut in pay; adequate income for the unemployed from paycheck to paycheck and for unsuccessful first-time job seekers; measures to curb the effects of plant closings; and, most important, conversion from military to civilian spending as a means of financing the program.

Our families cannot be saved unless we manage to preserve our right to earn a decent living under conditions of equality and unless we can exercise our right to make political decisions in the electoral arena. Therefore, what is necessary is a program of jobs with peace and affirmative action, democratic nationalization of basic industry and of the military-industrial complex, and the halting of racist assaults on Black people's political rights. This is the only framework within which practical programs addressing specific problems of Black families will have any hope for success.

Observers of the current crisis within the Black family might find it instructive to examine the present situation in some of the socialist countries such as the U.S.S.R. and the German Democratic Republic that are also experiencing a rapid growth in the number of single-parent families. In those countries, there is no semblance whatsoever of the soaring poverty associated with the increase in such families in the United States. If we as Black people in the United States want to guarantee that the dream for a better life is realized through our children, we must recognize the importance of setting our sights on a socialist future.

NOTES

1. Lorraine Hansberry, *A Raisin in the Sun* (New York: Signet Books, 1966), p. 33.

2. *Black and White Children: The Key Facts*, Children's Defense Fund (1985), pp. 1–2.

3. George Gilder, *Wealth and Poverty* (New York: Basic Books, 1981), p. 115.

4. *Ibid.*, p. 123.

5. *State Of Black America: 1985*, National Urban League, New York, p. 2.

6. *The New York Times*, Nov. 20, 1983.

7. National Urban League. op. cit., p. 4.

8. *National Review*, June 15, 1984, p. 63.

9. Children's Defense Fund. op. cit., p. 19.

10. *The New York Times*, May 7, 1984.

11. *Ibid.*

12. *The New York Times*, June 2, 1985.

13. *Ibid.*

14. *Ibid.*

15. Martin Luther King, Jr., *Where Do We Go from Here: Chaos or Community?* (New York: Bantam Books, 1968), p. 129.

16. *The New York Times*, May 7, 1984.

17. *Ebony*, Mar. 1985, p. 80.

18. *The New York Times*, June 2, 1985.

19. *The Women's Budget*, The Women's International League for Peace and Freedom. New York (June 1985).

20. *Ibid.*

Women in the 1980's:
Setbacks and Victories

As the UN Decade for Women (1976–85) came to a close, it was becoming increasingly evident that women worldwide constitute a political force capable of posing a compelling threat to the global forces of backwardness and oppression. Women in the Soviet Union and in other socialist countries who have organized impressive peace movements are demonstrating that we can generate a formidable united offensive against the nuclear-arms race. In South Africa, Nicaragua, and Palestine, women have been prominent and enthusiastic participants in their peoples' national-liberation struggles. Furthermore, the deepening consciousness of women in the United States and other capitalist countries accentuates the need for the radical socioeconomic changes that will guarantee full equality for all women.

Historically, when the women's movement has veered away from the path leading toward genuine equality for *all*

—Preface to the Soviet edition of *Women, Race & Class* (Moscow: Progress Publishers, 1987).

women, it has often been because of the deleterious and distorting influence of racist and antiworking-class ideas on the vision of feminist leaders. Throughout the history of the campaign for women's rights, there has been a tendency to isolate women's issues from the agendas of racially and nationally oppressed people and from the cause of the working class as a whole. Consequently, the indispensable role of Afro-American women and of working-class women of all racial backgrounds—Communist women, in particular—in determining many of the strategies and tactics of the campaign for women's equality has been largely omitted from the historical records.

During Ronald Reagan's two terms in office, women suffered critical setbacks in our quest for equality. While chipping away at the achievements of the women's movement thus far, the Reagan administration simultaneously conducted concerted attacks on the labor movement and on the rights of Afro-Americans, Latinos, Native Americans, Asians, and Pacific Islanders. The backdrop for this offensive was the increasingly dangerous militarization of the U.S. economy, epitomized by recent plans for the nuclearization of outer space. In attempts to justify this unprecedented escalation of the nuclear-arms race, the Reagan administration has repeatedly conjured up the historically debunked notion of the "Communist threat." Furthermore, its belligerent posture toward the struggles of people in Central America, Southern Africa, and the Middle East has been barely camouflaged by a shroud of anti-Soviet propaganda.

The reactionary forces that shaped Ronald Reagan's regressive policies have perpetuated dangerously high levels of unemployment and homelessness, a social climate promoting racist violence, and increased discrimination against

women. At the same time, however, their actions have
served to stimulate a massive anti-Reagan upsurge. Within
the women's movement, in particular, a growing awareness
has evolved of the interconnectedness of sexism, racism,
and the exploitation of the working class. And, most important, there is an expanding awareness of the insepara-
bility of women's issues from the quest for peace. In a
document submitted to the United Nations Conference and
Nongovernmental Forum at the end of the UN Decade for
Women, the Women's Coalition made the following asser-
tion:

> The status of women in the United States is not improving:
> *our status is deteriorating.* Racist, sexist, anti-labor and Cold
> War rhetoric and policies are used to justify militarization
> and exploitation and to divide and weaken us. Institution-
> alized racism and sexism distort social relations and under-
> mine our struggle for economic and political equality.
> Neither economic nor social development, nor women's
> equality can be achieved while our society is burdened with
> massive military budgets and our children, our families, and
> our own lives are threatened with nuclear holocaust.
>   The Women's Coalition for Nairobi recognizes that racial
> and international unity are essential to secure the needs of all
> women. As U.S. women, we struggle for our equality, eco-
> nomic development, and above all, world peace.[1]

More than ever before, it is incumbent upon women in
the United States to study the lessons—past as well as present, negative as well as positive—that emerge from the experiences of women in the Soviet Union. The dramatic
strides that have been made toward the social, economic,
and political equality of Soviet women have resulted from

revolutionary societal reorganization in accordance with the needs and aspirations of the working class. Like racial and national discrimination, sexism is an obstacle to socialist development and to the eventual advent of communism. And Soviet women, who will never forget the agony of Hitler's war against their people, persistently remind us that the fight for global peace must be an integral and enduring part of the quest for women's equality.

NOTES

1. *The Effects of Racism and Militarization on Women's Equality* (New York: Women for Racial and Economic Equality, 1985).

ON
INTERNATIONAL
ISSUES

When a Woman Is
a Rock: Reflections on
Winnie Mandela's Autobiography

They always put their hands
on the women first
they do this for a living
they do it to make a point
cutting away the heart
always leaves a hole
big enough for bullets
to crawl through

they strike
the gentle angry women
first
and when they do
they do not know
they are touching rock[1]

Where does a woman find the tenacity and resilience to
endure more than two decades of unrelenting efforts by an

—Originally published in *Vogue*, December 1985.

avowedly racist government to shatter her commitment to
her people's freedom or, barring that, to drive her toward
the brink of insanity? After innumerable jailings, house arrests, and bannings, after several nearly successful attempts
on her life and repeated episodes of harassment, Winnie
Mandela has emerged seemingly unscathed. At forty-nine,
the wife of Nelson Mandela—the imprisoned leader of the
African National Congress of South Africa—has been
clearly tempered by her ordeals. Yet she retains a gentleness
that endears her to most who are fortunate enough to encounter her. In 1985, on Ted Koppel's *Nightline*, millions
of television viewers caught a fleeting glimpse of this woman's spiritual beauty and political eloquence. Now, thanks
to Anne Benjamin, who edited a book entitled *Part of My
Soul Went with Him*, consisting of interviews, letters, and
testimonies by and about Winnie Mandela, it is possible to
become more intimately acquainted with her—with the person, the leader, and the remarkable symbol of the incisive
contemporary challenge to South African apartheid.

I am only seven years younger than Winnie Mandela. I
feel I have known her for a very long time. As a teenager
coming of age in Birmingham, Alabama, which was known
in some circles as "the Johannesburg of the South," I was
shocked to discover that elsewhere in the world, Black people were subjected to the same injustices of segregation as
we were in the southern United States. By the time I learned
of the existence of the African National Congress, Nelson
Mandela was already in prison. In 1977, shortly after she
was banished to Brandfort as a result of her leadership role
during the Soweto uprising, I listened to a taped telephone
conversation with Winnie Mandela. Since then, I have been
haunted by that voice, its tone of quiet determination, its

expressions of confidence in imminent victory for democracy in South Africa. Periodically, I have found myself constructing imaginary scenarios of her day-to-day existence. When I learned of the publication of *Part of My Soul*, I rejoiced.

Today, I feel more awed than ever, and more humbled by this proud-hearted woman's account of her unceasing battles with the apartheid regime. Having spent what seemed to be an interminable seventeen months in jail myself as I awaited trial on politically motivated charges, I was utterly devastated by Winnie Mandela's account of her experiences in prison, which caused the memories of my own incarceration to pale in comparison.

> In those days all I had in the cell was a sanitary bucket, a plastic bottle which could contain only three glasses of water and a mug. . . .
> . . . For a bed there was only a mat and three stinking filthy blankets. I rolled one up for a pillow and slept with the other two.
> The days and nights become so long that I found I was talking to myself. It is deathly quiet—that alone is a torture. You don't know what to do with yourself; you sit down, you stand up, you pace up and down . . . You lie on your stomach, you lie on your back, on your side; your body becomes sore because you are not used to sleeping on cement.
> (p. 99)

And I had complained fifteen years ago that in order to write on the tiny desk in my New York cell, it was necessary to sit on a malodorous toilet. Yet I had a desk as well as a toilet! And I had books, a legal pad, and a pencil (even as I complained because pens were banned from the cells). Each time I felt mice and roaches crawling across my body, I shuddered with disgust, while Winnie Mandela was over-joyed one day to find two ants in her bare cell. For her, these two living creatures broke the tormenting monotony of seventeen months of solitary confinement. During the course of my own imprisonment, I was physically assaulted only once. Winnie Mandela was brutally beaten so many times that she stopped counting. On one occasion, she was interrogated continuously for five days and five nights.

According to African tradition, one's name is supposed to capture the essence of one's being. In the Xhosa language, Winnie Mandela's African name, Nomzamo, means "trial"—"those who in their life will go through many trials" (p. 50). Between 1962 and 1985, she experienced only ten months of "freedom." The rest of the time she spent in prison, facing court charges, under house arrest, or banned. Moreover, ". . . her house was broken into; a petrol bomb was hurled through a window; her watchdog was poisoned; and one night three men broke in and attempted to strangle her" (p. 98).

What is the source of this woman's unrelenting courage? Perhaps her reflections on her childhood provide a clue.

> When I was a child, I thought then we owned all. The free-dom you have as a child, those undulating plains [of the Transkei], beautiful greenery—how we would run from one end of the river to the other, running over rolling beautiful green hills. I thought that was my country . . . [t]hen . . . when you grow up . . . a white man tells you that your own country doesn't belong to you, and that you must have a piece of paper to stay there . . . (p. 127)

When she married Nelson Mandela in 1958, she knew well that she had "married the struggle, the liberation of my people" (p. 65). Until 1964, when her husband was sentenced to life imprisonment following the Rivonia trials of the ANC leadership under the Suppression of Communism Act, she saw him only sporadically, and always clandestinely. Their two children, Zindzi and Zeni, learned to know their father during rare, always closely monitored prison visits. In May of 1984, Winnie was able to touch her husband for the first time in twenty years. It seems that with her unshakable political commitment, she has tapped a limitless well of emotional strength.

In South Africa, there are 4.3 million whites, 18.6 million Blacks, and 3.1 million people of mixed and Asian backgrounds. Blacks cannot vote; the majority of them have been stripped of citizenship in their own country and assigned to remote, barren areas designated as their "homelands" by the apartheid government. To work in the "white areas" (87 percent of the entire country), they must carry "passes." Major U.S. transnational corporations and banks, such as IBM, General Motors, and Bank of America, have invested heavily in the South African economy and have been instrumental in the administration of apartheid. As a direct consequence of the activist campaigns for divestment, however, scores of corporations have been compelled to pull out of South Africa, and cities, states, union pension funds, and other institutions have created investment portfolios from which businesses with South African interests have been barred.

Black South Africans and their white allies are posing their most intense and most organized challenge to the white minority government in their centuries-long history of struggle. At the same time, American public opinion is rapidly turning against the policies of the Botha regime—and consequently against the Reagan administration's strategy of "constructive engagement" with South Africa.

Part of My Soul Went with Him should be read by everyone who is concerned about the situation in South Africa—from those who have been abruptly awakened from their slumber by the televised sight of South African policemen training their weapons on Black children, to seasoned political activists who are immersed in anti-apartheid organizing. Although the structure of the book sometimes leaves something to be desired, its inestimable value resides in the fact that Winnie Mandela is allowed to plead her own case and to emerge as an eloquent, compelling spokesperson for her people.

Whoever might be disturbed by the involvement of the African National Congress in armed resistance should read her persuasive analysis of the limitations of nonviolence under circumstances where peacefully demonstrating schoolchildren are indiscriminately killed by machine-gun wielding police. Whoever might be under the impression that Black people in South Africa view their struggle as a race war—and are determined to exorcise their country of white people altogether—should read Winnie Mandela's tributes to white as well as Black women and men who have kept the flames of struggle burning for many decades. They should also seriously reflect on her vision of a free South Africa, based on the enfranchisement of Black people and on a multiracial democracy.

When Nelson Mandela is unconditionally released from prison—he has repeatedly rejected the freedom offered him by the government on the condition that he renounce the

African National Congress and its forceful tactics of resistance—and when Black people finally receive the franchise, he will no doubt be the undisputed choice of the electoral majority for prime minister. At that moment, Nomzomo Winnie Mandela will also take her place at the helm of a Free South Africa.

NOTES

1. Nicky Finney, "South Africa: When a Woman Is a Rock," in *Catalyst*, Fall 1986, vol. 1.

Children First:
The Campaign for
a Free South Africa

It is an immense honor for me to share this platform with such great anti-apartheid leaders as Archbishop Trevor Huddleston and the courageous president of the African National Congress, Oliver Tambo. My deepest gratitude goes to the organizers of this monumental conference, who have made it possible to for us to hear, in this liberated country of Zimbabwe, the voices of the children of South Africa. For it is the children who represent the future and who embody the spirit of democracy and freedom in their land.

My participation in this conference has given me cause to reflect upon my own experiences as a child, growing up in the segregated southern U.S. city of Birmingham, Alabama. It was there that I first learned about apartheid, for Birmingham was known in some progressive circles as "the Johannesburg of the South." In that city, in the early 1960's, four young Black girls who were close friends of mine were

—Address to the International Conference on Children, Repression, and the Law in Apartheid South Africa, Harare, Zimbabwe, September 27, 1987.

murdered by the Ku Klux Klan as they prayed in a church that was bombed one Sunday morning. Some people may be hesitant to believe that a government can assail, with systematic brutality, the children of oppressed people. However, I know from personal experience that when racism is in power, the children suffer as much as and often far more than those of us who feel that we are its most deeply wounded victims.

Even as South African children suffer, their spirit of resistance remains indomitable. This has been confirmed over and over again by their testimony during this conference. A speaker at one of the sessions put it this way: "The children of South Africa refuse to adjust to apartheid." When the children refuse to adjust to apartheid, we know that victory is just over the horizon. South Africa will be free! Namibia will be free!

We have learned as this conference has unfolded of children's experiences that are unimaginably more horrifying than anything most adults might ever encounter during an entire lifetime. Sixteen-year-olds are arrested and subjected to electric-shock torture. Yet a boy who described such torture in vivid detail concluded his testimony by expressing his desire to return to his country in order to resume his participation in the struggle for his people's liberation. There is incontrovertible evidence of a spirit among the children that refuses to be broken.

In every culture, it is true that youth is unencumbered by inhibitions. In South Africa, children are uninhibited even by war. The absence of inhibition in these children, however, is not equivalent to the usual naïveté that is the basis of most children's fearlessness. For naïveté is the product of an innocent ignorance of the consequences of one's actions. And these children, though they may be innocent, know all too well the consequences of their actions. They have seen their friends and relatives gunned down before their very eyes. They have seen their schoolmates attacked by ferocious police dogs. Indeed, the Black children of South Africa are fully cognizant of the fact that there is a constant danger of death looming over them. And yet they continue to resist. And they continue to sing and dance, keeping alive their undaunted belief in imminent freedom, even though the police have broken up such gatherings and have shot young people in the back as they have fled. As the offensive of the government and its henchmen grows increasingly violent, so the wills of the children become ever stronger.

Their resistance is awe-inspiring. But let us not forget that they are children. Let us not forget that they are the future. Let us remember with every breath we take that apartheid is soon to be nothing more than a thing of the past. And let us remember, above all else, that it is our duty and responsibility to assist those who are surely moving to abolish the archaic apartheid system and to save South Africa's up-and-coming leaders. For they are, after all, still children.

International public opinion must proclaim with a resounding, united voice to the criminal Botha regime: "End the war against the children!"

Those of us who are here from the United States represent many thousands of anti-apartheid activists among our people. We and our comrades at home find it outrageous that while the entire international community has denounced apartheid as a murderous, criminal violation of human rights, the Reagan administration has audaciously continued to bolster the Botha regime with its policy of constructive engagement. In actuality, the relationship has gone far beyond the "engagement" phase. Botha and Reagan have been united in unholy, destructive matrimony.

In an attempt to justify their posture, Reagan and the corporate monopolies whose interests he represents conjure up the specter of communism. In fact, the entire foreign policy of the Reagan administration has been saturated through and through with anticommunism and anti-Sovietism.

We pose these questions to Ronald Reagan: Is communism responsible for the atrocities in South Africa? Who, in truth, is the real enemy of people's quests for freedom throughout the world? Who, in truth, is responsible for the nuclear threat which looms over the very future of humanity?

The propagandists of Reaganism continue to disseminate a distorted picture of the South African struggle. They pretend that the contest in South Africa is over the issue of racial segregation—that it is a civil-rights reform movement and nothing more. They thus try to conceal the fact that what is transpiring in South Africa is a struggle for democracy. *All* the people of South Africa want to participate in the process of determining their country's destiny. It is a fight for national liberation, for economic and political power. It is a revolutionary fight for democracy.

We from the United States reaffirm in your presence that Reagan does not represent our people any more than Botha represents the people of South Africa. In the United States, over five thousand people have been arrested during the last period for protesting apartheid. Twenty states and sixty-five cities have divested over $7 billion. As a direct consequence of our activism, U.S. investment in South Africa has been cut in half. Nonetheless, we know that there are corporations that have ostensibly pulled out of South Africa while continuing to finance apartheid by using other channels to supply the government with goods, services, and technology.

We therefore say that all economic relationships with South Africa must be broken! We want mandatory comprehensive sanctions! We also demand the release of Nelson Mandela and all political prisoners—men, women, and children alike! We say stop the executions of our sisters and brothers and their children!

And we promise you, our South African sisters and brothers who have come from both within and without the country, that we will immediately work to build an expansive and militant campaign to save the young ones from further repression, brutalization, torture, and death.

End the war against the children of South Africa!

Amandla Ngawethu! (Power to the People!)

Finishing the Agenda: Reflections on Forum '85, Nairobi, Kenya

Although I very much treasure my opportunities to travel abroad, I always anxiously anticipate the journey home. The sense of completion associated with the return trip naturally complements the excitement of having visited another country and experienced its culture. Yet as I stood on line in the Nairobi airport in the summer of 1985, preparing to board the departing plane, I instinctively hesitated to acknowledge that my African pilgrimage had come to an end. Why, I wondered, was I so reluctant to leave this city that was the site of the international assembly marking the climax of the United Nations Decade for Women? By the time I secured my belongings in the luggage compartment and settled as comfortably as possible into my assigned seat on the plane, I realized that my reluctance to leave this African city emanated from my disappointment that the UN Decade for Women was drawing to a close.

From July 10–19, thousands of women representing the world's multitudinous nations, cultures, and ethnic groups had celebrated the culmination of ten years of intense international activism on behalf of our rights as women. But for most of the masses of women on the planet, the international epoch of conscious challenges to the age-old oppression of male supremacy had only just begun. And, indeed, my own experiences throughout those two weeks abundantly confirmed the fact that we had finally created a firm foundation—but only a foundation—for a more influential and more politically mature international women's movement. Although Forum '85, as well as the official UN End of the Decade for Women Conference, grew out of a tradition forged over decades of progressive international women's gatherings, it was the first assembly to take place at a time when world public opinion is finally acknowledging the legitimacy of women's quest for equality.

The global movement for women's emancipation is finally becoming cognizant of the links between our struggles as women and the worldwide opposition to capitalist exploitation, racist oppression, and the nuclear militarization that threatens the future of humankind. For those who attended the 1975 Mexico City convocation and the 1980 mid-decade meeting in Copenhagen, the composition of the Nairobi gathering was qualitatively different. This was the first time in the history of international women's conferences that the majority of the participants were women of color. For those of us who have grown accustomed to being designated "minorities" because we are people of color living in Europe and North America, the Nairobi experience reaffirmed a basic historical reality: If indeed we happen to be in the minority on some of the world's continents, globally we constitute the majority of the human population.

As an Afro-American woman, I felt especially proud that the numbers of Black women from the United States in attendance at the Nongovernmental (NGO) Forum in Nairobi were greater than at all previous international gatherings. While prominent women like Mary Church Terrell during the first half of the century and Vinie Burrows in more recent years have been powerful voices for Afro-American women at global women's assemblies, this time more than a thousand Black American women participated in the Nairobi deliberations. We led workshops on the ties between racism and sexism, we shared our cultural heritages through song, dance, and poetry of resistance, we demonstrated our solidarity with our South African, Nicaraguan, and Palestinian sisters, and we joined in dialogues with our sisters from the socialist countries, concurring with their urgent message that we must all fight for world peace. Every day we spontaneously joined our sisters from Africa, Asia, South America, Europe, Australia, and the Middle East in militant and celebratory dance rhythms and chants on the great lawn. As an Afro-American woman, I sensed that the more than one thousand of us present in Nairobi were breaking new ground for our sisters and brothers at home. We were exploring the global sociohistorical conditions of our own oppression, and we were building new bridges linking us to the defiant women, the militant workers, the struggling peoples and the progressive, peace-loving nations of the world.

I participated in the NGO Forum in Nairobi as an activist in the multiracial organization Women for Racial and Economic Equality (WREE). In the New York metropolitan area, WREE initiated the formation of the Women's Coalition for Nairobi, embracing the Women's International League for Peace and Freedom, the Coalition for Labor Union Women, and many other women's groups. By virtue of WREE's affiliation with the Women's International Democratic Federation (WIDF), a UN nongovernmental organization, we were able to present an extensive document, entitled "The Effects of Racism and Militarization on Women," to the official UN conference. Our sisters distributed several thousand copies of the document to the women attending the forum, and WREE leaders conducted a workshop for the purpose of explaining its content. During the first days of the forum, we decided to formulate a petition reflecting the thrust of the document, to be circulated among the U.S. women attending the forum. The signatures would later be presented to the official U.S. governmental delegation to the United Nations conference.

The official U.S. delegation was headed by Ronald Reagan's daughter Maureen, who had hardly distinguished herself as a sincere advocate for women's equality. She may have supported the demands of politically conservative, economically secure white women, but she has never represented working-class women, and certainly not Black, Latina, Native American, Asian, and Pacific Island women. As a mouthpiece for her father, himself a figurehead for the most antiworking-class, sexist, racist, and indeed most militaristic sectors of the capitalist monopolies, Maureen Reagan intentionally misconstrued the status and struggles of the masses of women in our country. She assumed the posture that, like Zionism and apartheid, racism—and indeed the halting of the nuclear-arms race—are not "authentic" women's issues.

When Maureen Reagan delivered her opening address at the official UN conference, she proclaimed that women in the United States are well on their way to emancipation. In fact, she said that "all barriers to political equality have long since been eliminated." The four main issues relating to the sexist oppression of women in our country, she said, are "women refugees, women in development, literacy, and domestic violence." Certainly these issues have their place on women's agenda, but when they are presented as the only truly important questions defining women's oppression in the United States, they fundamentally distort our situation. What about racism? What about unemployment and economic inequities? And, indeed, what about militarization?

The four issues chosen by Maureen Reagan were evoked for the express purpose of diverting attention away from the larger context of women's inequality. During the official conference, delegation leaders from the United States at times had difficulty recalling the Reagan line of reasoning. At one of the press conferences, for example, Lois Harrington, a member of the Reagan delegation, attempted to enumerate the administration's four categories: "Domestic violence, literacy, development and . . . —oh, Alan [referring to Alan Keyes, the main negotiator for the U.S. delegation], you'll have to help me, I can't remember the fourth." When Keyes screamed out, "Refugees," Harrington responded, "Oh, yes, how could I forget? We have so many refugees."

Our petition called upon the official U.S. delegation to support two documents, the U.N. Convention on the Elimination of Discrimination Against Women and the Declaration on the Participation of Women in Promoting World Peace and Cooperation. We further demanded the reduction of the military budget and the utilization of the released funds for the general progress of our people and specifically for the achievement of women's equality. As the conduct of transnational corporations adversely affects women's economic status, we demanded that their activities be restricted. Moreover, women's economic independence and participation in the trade-union movement are key factors in our quest for equality. Therefore, we called for guarantees for equal pay for work of comparable value to that performed by men as well as the right to full employment and a guaranteed income. We demanded that racial oppression of women—as well as men—be eliminated, and that the rights of foreign and undocumented workers be secured. We lent our support to all measures that seek to improve the quality of life for all women, including the control of police brutality, decent housing, health care, and quality education.

As the petition proclaimed, sexual violence must be eliminated and women's right to choose in matters of sexuality must be ensured. Economic, social, and legislative guarantees must be created for full reproductive rights, including abortion, freedom from forced sterilization, access to birth control, childbearing, primary health care, infant care, child care, paid maternity leave, and job and pension guarantees. We called for aid to women in Southern Africa, Central America, the Middle East, and throughout the world who are fighting for their people's democratic rights and national independence. And finally, our petition urged that we all work for world peace by halting U.S. intervention and aggression, withdrawing all nuclear missiles, negotiating bilateral arms-control agreements, and especially by ending the present Star Wars research designed to militarize outer space.

More than 65 percent of the U.S. women attending the forum and conference signed this petition: We gathered over thirteen hundred signatures from the two thousand U.S.

women in Nairobi. Among the signers were Dorothy Height, president of the National Council of Negro Women; Emagene Walker, executive board member of the Coalition of Labor Union Women; Vinie Burrows, WIDF representative to the United Nations and international vice-president of WREE; Erma Henderson, the Black woman who is president of the Detroit City Council; Vivian Lowry, civil rights leader; Lydia Martinez, clergywoman in the United Methodist Church; and Edith George, Native American leader in the United Methodist Church.

Forum '85 was indeed a historic experience for women from the United States, for it revealed that we are beginning to understand that an enormous potential resides with us. If we forge and consolidate a united, multiracial, antimonopoly women's movement, we will soon have earned the righteous solidarity of our fighting sisters in Nicaragua, Iran, and South Africa.

Women in Egypt:
A Personal View

In 1973, I passed through Cairo en route to Brazzaville to celebrate the tenth anniversary of the Congolese Revolution. I remember how frustrated I felt then, spending time in Egypt, yet being unable because of time constraints to catch even a fleeting glimpse of that country's life. Twelve years later, as I waited to clear customs, I thought about the women in Africa and, indeed, the many thousands of women all over the world who, like their sisters in Egypt, were preparing to celebrate the end of the UN Decade for Women in Nairobi. I experienced the invigoration of feeling myself a participant in a vastly expanding global women's movement within which my Third World sisters were finally beginning to receive the respect they deserved.

When I arrived in Cairo, three women representing the newly established Arab Women's Solidarity Association (AWSA), which had agreed to host my visit, were waiting

—Originally published in *Women: A World Report*, New York: Oxford University Press, 1985.

at the airport to receive me. Since TWA had lost my luggage (which I did not retrieve until the night before returning home), we were quickly on our way to the hotel in Giza. As we traveled through the city, I was unexpectedly shaken by the sight of unending rows of small sand-colored mausoleums that spread across a vast and ancient cemetery. I was told by my hosts that this enormous city of the dead also housed at least a million living beings. So critical is the housing shortage in Cairo that people are forced to seek refuge in shelters that have been constructed for the dead members of their families. I was immediately sensitized to the fact that the issue of adequate housing was high on the list of priorities for women in Egypt.

When I initially agreed to travel to Egypt for the purpose of documenting my experiences with women there, I did not yet know that the sponsors of this project expected me to focus specifically on issues relating to the sexual dimension of women's pursuit of equality. I was not aware, for example, that the practice of clitoridectomy was among the issues I would be asked to discuss. Since I was very much aware of the passionate debate still raging within international women's circles around the efforts of some Western feminists to lead a crusade against female circumcision in African and Arab countries, once I was informed about the particular emphasis of my visit, I seriously reconsidered proceeding with the project.

As an Afro-American woman familiar with the sometimes hidden dynamics of racism, I had previously questioned the myopic concentration on female circumcision in U.S. feminist literature on African women. The insinuation seems frequently to be made that the women in the twenty or so countries where this outmoded and dangerous practice occurs would magically ascend to a state of equality once they managed to throw off the fetters of genital mutilation—or rather, once white Western feminists (whose appeals often suggest that this is the contemporary "white woman's burden") accomplished this for them. As the Association of African Women for Research and Development pointed out:

> This new crusade of the West has been led out of the moral and cultural prejudices of Judaeo-Christian Western Sociology: aggressiveness, ignorance or even contempt, paternalism and activism are the elements which have infuriated and then shocked many people of good will. In trying to reach their own public, the new crusaders have fallen back on sensationalism, and have become insensitive to the dignity of the very women they want to "save." They are totally unconscious of the latent racism which such a campaign evokes in countries where ethnocentric prejudice is so deep-rooted. And in their conviction that this is a "just cause," they have forgotten that these women from a different race and a different culture are also *human beings*, and that solidarity can only exist alongside self-affirmation and mutual respect.[1]

The dynamics here are not entirely dissimilar from those characterizing the historical campaign waged by U.S. feminists for the right to birth control. It is easy to understand why that movement, as righteous as its intentions may have been, aroused hostility in Afro-American women, because it often portrayed us as bestial and oversexed, indiscriminantly reproducing in such numbers that the rule of the white majority might be ultimately challenged.

During the years in which I have lectured at various universities throughout the United States, I have encountered an astounding number of women who know virtually nothing about the situation of women in Egypt or in the Sudan, aside from the fact that they are victims of genital mutilation. It is indeed revealing that while these college students do not hesitate to express their disgust and horror at the idea of female circumcision, they rarely seem disturbed by the lengths to which some women in their own country will go in order to alter their bodies surgically for the purpose of conforming to male-supremacist standards of beauty. Moreover, they do not often recognize that they need to explore the larger picture of women's oppression in those countries before presuming to make authoritative observations about what should be done to eradicate this misogynist practice. Before departing for Egypt, I realized that I could not in good conscience write about genital mutilation and other examples of sexual oppression in Egypt without acknowledging the manipulation of these problems by those who fail to consider the importance of the larger economic-political context of male supremacy.

Considering the nature of my visit to Egypt, I was greatly disappointed to learn that Nawal El Saadawi, the internationally acclaimed feminist who is president of the AWSA, would be abroad during the time I spent in her country. Ironically, she was scheduled to deliver a series of lectures in the United States during the only period I had free from my teaching responsibilities to make the trip to Cairo. Since she planned to remain in the United States for an extended period, I arranged to meet with her upon my return. I had been introduced to her the previous year when she was lecturing in the San Francisco Bay Area, and, having been thoroughly impressed by her personality as well as her brilliant writings, I looked forward to seeing her again in New York.

The itinerary arranged by the AWSA was conceived in hopes of permitting me to make contact with as wide a range of women as possible. Included in the schedule were large, relatively formal meetings, small discussions, and individual interviews. Political leaders, social scientists, writers, artists, trade unionists, students, and peasant women were among the scores with whom I was to meet. When I sat down with my traveling companion to discuss the itinerary after our seventeen-hour plane trip and an unsuccessful attempt at an afternoon nap, my mind felt rather fuzzy, and I began momentarily to doubt whether it would be possible to absorb the vast amount of information I would receive over the coming days. I suggested to Debra that we rise early the next morning to take a walk along the Nile before breakfast. I hoped that some fresh air, exercise, and the spirit of the ancient river would clear my head before we submerged ourselves in the day's interviews and meetings.

But the stroll along the Nile gave me much more to think about than I had expected. As we commented on the contrast between the bareheaded women and those attired in a variety of veils, we stumbled upon a dusty, makeshift tent that was pitched on the riverbank in the middle of one of the city's busiest sections. Suddenly, out of the dark interior emerged two men who had obviously just woken from their night's sleep. My mind flashed back to the people who had set up their homes in the cemetery. This was the legacy of Sadat's open-door economic policy: the transnational corporations that had greedily rushed into Egypt under the guise of promoting economic development had created more unemployment, more poverty, and more homelessness. In one of the many meetings to take place during the coming days, this comment would be offered regarding the effects of poverty on sexual relations:

> Take a family here in Cairo with five or six children. They all live in the same room. If there are two sofas and a bed in the room, then with a child on each sofa, the mother and father will sleep on the bed and three children will sleep under the bed. Try to imagine the kind of sexual relationship the parents have under this pressure. Even though there are sexual problems, these problems are of secondary importance.

After breakfast, we crossed El Tahir Street, where our hotel was located, and walked a short distance to the apartment of Shahira Mehrez, one of the women who had greeted us at the airport the previous day. The secretary general of the AWSA, Mona Aboussena, was waiting to accompany us to the National Center for Sociological and Criminological Studies, where we immediately entered into discussions with a group of women who had already gathered in anticipation of our visit. As I had expected, the response to the description of the project I had undertaken was instantaneous and incisive. The most outspoken of the group, Dr. Shehida Elbaz, hastened to point out that the campaign against circumcision underway in the West had created the utterly false impression that this genital mutilation is the main feature of Muslim women's oppression. "Women in the West should know," she asserted,

> that we have a stand in relation to them concerning our issues and our problems. We reject their patronizing attitude. It is

connected with built-in mechanisms of colonialism and with their sense of superiority. Maybe some of them don't do it consciously, but it is there. They decide what problems we have, how we should face them, without even possessing the tools to know our problems.

Dr. Elbaz went on to describe a public debate she had attended in England, during which she challenged a number of women who argued that the eradication of female bodily mutilation was the pivotal issue in the quest for women's liberation in such countries as Egypt, the Sudan, and Somalia.

> I said to them, "But all my life I have lived in Cairo. I can't assume that I have the right to talk about women in the countryside without conducting field research. So how can you decide for us, so far away? You know nothing about our culture, our background, our level of development."

Having firmly declared her differences with the most-publicized proponents of the Western anticircumcision campaign, she generously shared with us some fascinating information on the recent historical evolution of attitudes toward sex in Egypt. Often recounting her own personal experiences, she always meticulously placed her observations in their respective economic and political contexts. Her remarks had a recurring theme: During the 1960's, prior to Sadat's government—and particularly before the Camp David Accords and the open-door policy—women were far freer from male tutelage than they are today. Women have suffered a retrenchment of economic, political, and even sexual oppression as a direct result of Egypt's new ties to the United States and Israel. I was impressed by this woman's frankness, and found myself feeling far more at ease than I originally had anticipated.

Perhaps I had begun to feel a bit too relaxed. After all, I had slipped into a cultural continuum whose acquaintance I had previously made through mental excursions alone. In any case, the events that transpired that evening during a dinner at Shahira Mehrez's home took me unawares. When Debra and I arrived, a good number of women were already there. At first, I tried to converse individually with several women about their work—and virtually everyone there was involved in some way in the effort to elevate women's status. Moving from one seat to another around a traditional circular brass table, I talked first to a sociology professor, then to a journalist, and afterward to the well-known artist and peace activist Inji Efflatoun, who presented me with a catalog containing a portrait she had painted of me during the period I spent in jail.

After more guests arrived, Mona Aboussena suggested that I formally address the thirty-five or so women who were attending the dinner. Prefacing my remarks with comments about the importance of the upcoming End of the Decade for Women Forum in Nairobi, I went on to say that I had been asked to make this trip—as other women from around the world were visiting a variety of countries—in order to write an article based on my experiences, brief though they would be, with women in Egypt. When I mentioned that the specific topic was "Women and Sex," and before I had time to explain the particular approach I planned to take, pandemonium erupted. The obvious hostility arising from every corner of the room made me regret not formulating my ideas in such a way as to avoid the spontaneous outrage that was apparently elicited by the very mention of the word *sex*.

I must have initially repressed my own emotional responses, because when I was finally able to get a word into the discussion, I reacted rather defensively. However, it soon became clear that the very idea that sex might be the focus of an article on Egyptian women was so objectionable that I could not stem the tide waters of anger simply by qualifying my own position on the subject. I labored to convince myself to refrain from attempting to defend my own position. After all, was I not in Egypt to learn about the way Egyptian women themselves interpreted the role of sexuality in their lives and their struggles? And was I not especially interested in their various responses to the unfortunate chauvinism characterizing attitudes in the capitalist countries toward the sexual dimension of Arab women's lives? I tried to persuade myself that even within these attacks, which seemed clearly directed at me, there was a significant lesson to be learned.

"Angela Davis in the Third World," said Dr. Latifa Zayat, to whom I had been previously introduced. She continued: "Your name, your personality, is known because of your struggle. You can be used by your society, a wealthy society, which is trying to exploit our country."

> I have come to see you this evening because you are Angela Davis. If you were simply an American research worker, I wouldn't have come to see you. I would have even boycotted this meeting, because I know that through this research we are being turned into animals, into guinea pigs. I would boycott any American who is doing research on Arab women because I know that we are being tested, we are being listed

in catalogs, we are being defined in terms of sexuality for reasons which are not in our own interests.

Dr. Zayat, a highly respected veteran leader in progressive causes, explained that she made those remarks so that I might better understand the reactions of the women. Eventually, another woman summed up the discussion by saying:

You would be doing a great service to the women's cause in the Third World if you tell people that women in the Third World refuse to be treated as sexual objects or as sexual experiments. We want to be liberated, we want to be emancipated, we want to be equal—but from an economic point of view, not from a sexual point of view.

I don't think she meant to dismiss altogether the importance of sexual equality. Rather, she seemed to be suggesting that an isolated challenge to sexual inequality would not solve the problems associated with women's state of economic dependency or their exclusion from the political process, not to mention the exploitation and poverty suffered by women and men alike.

In reflecting on the conversation that had transpired that evening, I began to wonder whether it would be possible within such a short period of time to move beyond discussions centering on the problematic posture of researchers from the capitalist countries dealing with issues of sexuality. Two days later, in a meeting convened at the headquarters of the Hoda Shaarawi Association, named after the founder of the Egyptian women's movement, there arose similarly intense reactions. Dr. Shehida Elbaz, whom I had previously interviewed, argued during this meeting that I should not have agreed to write—even critically—on the topic of sexuality.

> I am outraged by the assignment of these topics. Although you have defended yourself very well, it raises in my mind another question: the role of the revolutionary woman in the West. Because it is so obvious from this assignment that it reflects the international division of labor imposed on the Third World by the Western capitalist countries. To make the topic of England "Women and Politics," and in Egypt "Women and Sex," shows that they assume that women's participation in politics in England is more important than in Egypt. Whereas although women may be more involved in politics in England, in prospect and destination it is much less radical, much less revolutionary, and it does not threaten the international capitalist system.

It seemed to be the consensus of the gathering that the politics underlying the distribution of topics for this anthology—whether consciously or not—misrepresented the cause of Egyptian women. Why, indeed, was not sex investigated in England or in the United States? Did the prevalence of female circumcision or the widespread adoption of the veil among urban women indicate that the most salient features of women's oppression in Egypt were sexual? Or was it simply in the interests of sensationalism that this topic was suggested?

Several women, however—and a man as well—argued that sexuality cannot be ignored by those who authentically are concerned with the emancipation of women. The young man said very poignantly, "Women cannot become creative agents without being freed from sexual oppression." Dr.

Nadja Atef, to whom I was later introduced, spoke about Egyptian women's responsibility to confront and publicly represent their own positions on questions involving sexuality:

> The fact is, we must be sensitive to the question of sexuality. Otherwise we would not have argued so happily and for so long and totally forgotten to talk about other issues. In and of itself, this is a touchy area in our society, and I think we have to look at ourselves in order to find out what our responsibility is to represent ourselves. It may be our duty actually to write about this. It may be our duty to start putting forth our position at forums and to publishers abroad. If this topic upsets us, let us speak about it openly. Why does it upset us? Every time you say "sex," people respond as to a stimulus-response test—they go crazy.

After this comment, Nadja Atef received extended applause. Later that evening, when I spoke with Dr. Sheriff Hetata, Nawal el Saadawi's husband and frequent collaborator, I asked him to comment on the relationship between the sexual and political dimensions of Egyptian women's experience. His response was concrete and to the point. The sexual oppression imposed on so many women results, for example, in the prohibition of women's participation in political activities. "If you want to hold a political meeting for young women and the young women can't go out after seven o'clock in the evening, there is no meeting." As long as women are viewed as the sexual property of their present or future husbands, their ability to bring about the institutional transformations that will lessen the burden of sexist oppression will be severely limited. This dialectic condemns an isolated focus on sexual issues, but demands that these issues be considered as prerequisites for the larger struggle.

The overwhelming majority of the women with whom I spoke were urban, educated women. While many of them had come from poor village backgrounds, their life-styles were very much removed from those of the masses of Egyptian women. "I met a thirteen-year-old girl in Upper Egypt," one woman recounted, "and this girl said":

> As far as the government is concerned, I have not been born at all. I have no birth certificate. I do not go to school. I have no official document at all. I was born and I will die, but as far as the government is concerned, I'm not there. I have never been there.

The practice of female circumcision is gradually becoming obsolete in big cities like Cairo and Alexandria. However, the degree to which it is still prevalent in the country as a whole often goes unrecognized. Most of the women with whom I spoke were absolutely opposed to the practice of genital mutilation. Many of those of my generation and older who spoke about their own personal experiences said that they had themselves been circumcised, but that they had broken the cycle with their daughters. And, indeed, the young women I met—primarily students—had not suffered this practice at all.

In her pioneering work on Arab women, *The Hidden Face of Eve*, Nawal El Saadawi, who was one of the first to publicly raise the issue of female circumcision, described her own experience at six years of age. She was seized from her bed by family members, who she thought were thieves in the night, and taken to the bathroom, where the operation was performed.

> . . . I realized that my thighs had been pulled wide apart, and that each of my lower limbs was being held as far away from the other as possible, gripped by steel fingers that never relinquished their pressure. I felt that the rasping knife or blade was heading straight down toward my throat. Then suddenly the sharp metallic edge seemed to drop between my thighs and there cut off a piece of flesh from my body. I screamed with pain despite the tight hand held over my mouth, for the pain was not just a pain, it was like a searing flame that went through my whole body.[2]

Research conducted by Dr. Saadawi approximately ten years ago indicated that some 97.5 percent of uneducated families and 66.2 percent of educated families continued to sanction the performance of clitoridectomies on their daughters. I visited a village outside the city of Mansoura, and while I could not directly engage in conversations with the village inhabitants because of the language barrier, I was able indirectly to conduct a number of interviews. All of the five women with whom I had contact there had been circumcised. They were all in their twenties. This was one of the most difficult moments of my visit. The masses of women in Egypt are peasants, yet I had only a few hours to spend attempting to communicate with these women, whose language was completely unfamiliar to me. How could I honestly view these as anything more than token encounters? I thought about a book I had recently read, Nayra Atiya's collection of oral histories of Egyptian women from peasant backgrounds, entitled *Khul Khaal*. She is herself Egyptian, yet it took her five years to develop the material for this book, in which the women talk frankly about their lives and unabashedly present their own interpretations of such sexual-initiation rites as circumcision and defloration.

The key question, it seems—at least among progressive women and men—is not whether circumcision is an acceptable contemporary cultural practice, but rather how to initiate a viable strategy for relegating it to historical obsolescence. As Nawal El Saadawi has pointed out:

> [A]mputation of the clitoris and sometimes even of the external genital organs goes hand in hand with brainwashing of girls, with a calculated merciless campaign to paralyze their capacity to think and to judge and to understand. For down the ages a system has been built up which aims at destroying the ability of women to see the exploitation to which they are subjected, and to understand its causes.[3]

At least one woman with whom I spoke during my stay in Egypt was directly involved in a campaign against female circumcision: Azziza Hussein, president of the Family Planning Association. She has delivered papers on the subject at various international conferences, and attempts, throughout the family-planning network, to educate mothers and the midwives who perform circumcisions about the need to obliterate the practice. Perhaps because she is involved in direct action with respect to the dissemination of contraceptive measures, she also believes in direct-action campaigns to eradicate genital mutilation.

I am trying to do something about the problem, which reflects itself in so many ways in our society. We've studied it
and we are taking action. We are trying to reach those who
have the possibility of doing something about this practice,
which means the nurses, the midwives. We formed a national
committee in 1979. . . . The taboos that we have with regard
to sex, we've broken them because we've dealt with family
planning. This is why we are the ones who are able to tackle
female circumcision.

While Azziza Hussein aggressively advocated tackling the
problem head on, she would not consider isolating it from
its larger social context.

Even if it were possible to envision the success of an
isolated campaign targeting female bodily mutilation, the
fact that Egyptian women represent barely 10 percent of the
labor force would remain unchanged. That 71 percent of
the female population suffers from illiteracy would be unaltered. The personal status of women with respect to polygamy, divorce, and guardianship would remain one of
socially enforced powerlessness.

Actually, the relationship between this salient sexual issue
and the socioeconomic elements of women's oppression is
one in which the former is clearly conditioned by the latter.
It is not really possible to foresee the universal abolition of
female circumcision unless the process of integrating women
into the labor force moves forward, unless the female literacy rate is significantly raised, and unless the personal
status of women within the family is elevated. These specific
changes in the condition of women cannot themselves be
considered in isolation from far-reaching transformations in

the society as a whole: economic development and progressive social change, which would indeed fundamentally
alter the lives of women as well as men in Egypt.

Many women whom I encountered emphasized the centrality of the current struggle to defend the status of women
within Egyptian family law. The series of amendments to
the law on personal status approved by the National Assembly in 1979 marked the first changes in this area to have
occurred in fifty years. At issue was a man's unilateral right
to divorce his wife and to engage in the practice of multiple
marriages, thus his right to openly treat women as sexual
property. The amendments did not change the husband's
right to obtain a divorce from his wife at will—and without
having to go through the courts—but it did provide that
the wife be immediately informed of the divorce. Likewise,
while the man retained his right to marry up to four wives—
as is his prerogative according to the Sharia (Muslim law)—
he was compelled by the amendments to inform his present
wife or wives of his intentions and any future wife of his
marital status.

Obviously, the fundamental inequality of the woman
within the family remained unaltered. Nevertheless, there
are presently efforts under way, encouraged by Islamic fun-
damentalist elements, to repeal the new law on the grounds
that it is unconstitutional. If this occurs, those meager rights
women have managed to acquire in relation to marriage
would be nullified. Divorced women would no longer be
entitled to alimony amounting to two years' maintenance
(or more if the marriage was especially long), but rather for
one year, as was the case prior to the amendments. Moreover, a divorced woman who retains custody of her children

would no longer be guaranteed the right to living quarters, which presently must be provided by her ex-husband. She would be forced out of the home she had previously shared with her husband and would once again be compelled to seek shelter under her parents' roof. Women's right to sue for divorce, while it is by no means comparable to men's corresponding right, became less rigidly restricted with the enactment of the 1979 amendments. Now, there is a nine-month waiting period during which the court attempts to mediate, and in the event that this attempt fails, the divorce is finalized. Men seeking divorce face no waiting period. The amendments also extended age limits of child custody for the wife, previously seven for boys and nine for girls, with possible extensions to nine and eleven, respectively. Presently, according to the amendments, custody is automatically given to the mother until the boy is nine and the girl eleven, subject to extensions of fifteen for male children and until marriage for female children.

Azziza Hussein pointed to the amendments' important implications for women's ability to move toward economic independence.

> Another important and new aspect of the amendments is the confirmation of the woman's right to work. This right is not contingent any more on the husband's approval. In the past, a woman who worked against her husband's wishes was legally placed in the category of *nashez*, meaning "disobedient." As such, she lost her right to maintenance by her husband, who had the right to neglect her. The wife's right to a court divorce was very much jeopardized by the "disobedient" status.[4]

AWSA had recently organized a meeting of representatives from various political parties in order to pressure Parliament to reject the fundamentalists' bill. However, as Nawal El Saadawi has pointed out, although they opposed the new bill, they were hardly satisfied with the 1979 amendments. If women are to move in the direction of achieving an equal status within the family, polygamy must be outlawed altogether, and women must have equal rights to divorce. Moreover, as many women emphasized, women must eventually be capable of achieving economic equality if they wish to enjoy equality in their personal status.

As far as women's role within the family is concerned, important structural changes are occurring as a result of the migration of Egyptian labor abroad. About 2 million Egyptians are working abroad, primarily in the Gulf countries, among whom are men from the working and peasant classes. As Sheriff Hetata pointed out, for the first time in the history of Egypt, large numbers of married men are leaving their families to go abroad for reasons other than military service:

> The women take over the responsibilities of looking after the fields and responsibilities within the family as a whole. Because the men are not present, the women are becoming the decision-makers. Therefore, when they return, there are often serious problems in the relationships.

Certainly this economic phenomenon must be affecting the structure of sexual dominance within the family.

On several occasions, I asked about the prevalence of rape in Egypt and was told that in recent years there has been a rising incidence of sexual assault. However, there was a

universal response of incredulity when I shared in one meeting some statistics regarding the incidence of sexual assault
in the United States. Aamina Shafix, a journalist and leading
member of the Progressive Unionist party, tied the rising
incidence of rape in Egypt to the overall deterioration of
the status of women since the end of the Nasser era and
specifically to the dissemination of such capitalist cultural
commodities as pornography. Rape is a capital offense in
Egypt, but cases against rapists are frequently dismissed on
the grounds that the victims are sexually promiscuous.
Mona Aboussena told me about a recent case of a woman
who was raped by four men who also stole her money. The
case was dismissed because of the "conditions of the
woman," meaning that she was considered to be either a
professional prostitute or "sexually familiar" with men.
This problem, of course, is hardly peculiar to Egypt or to
the Arab world. The dualistic representation of women as
virgins and whores is an integral element of the ideology
of womanhood associated with the Judeo-Christian tradition.

Among the young urban population—and especially
among students—social attitudes regarding the status of
women, which have undergone some superficial changes in
the capitalist countries, are beginning to be problematic. As
the need for a woman to prove that she is a virgin at marriage
is increasingly questioned, women suffer from the clash between emerging values and the established culture. Although dismantling this double standard with respect to
women's right to engage in premarital sex is one of the
prerequisites for women's social emancipation, during this
transitional period, women are often lured into relationships
on the pretense of encouraging them to express their sexual

freedom, only to discover later that their partners do not wish to marry them because they are no longer virgins. Young women of the petty bourgeoisie therefore often feel compelled to undergo surgery to repair the hymen in order to be considered suitable candidates for marriage.

There is indeed a great danger of representing sexual liberation as "women's liberation," as women of my generation came to recognize in the United States during the 1960's. Precisely as a result of the widespread dissemination of the Pill, women were represented as moving in the direction of sexual liberation. Actually, they suffered disguised sexual exploitation, because if they took the Pill, wishing to avoid becoming pregnant was no longer a valid excuse for not having sex. It is not coincidental that the women's liberation movement erupted directly on the heels of the so-called "sexual revolution."

As reliance on birth-control measures becomes more widespread in Egypt, and especially since this is occurring within the context of an omnipresent cultural invasion from the Western capitalist countries, problems relating to the sexual conduct of young women will no doubt increase in severity. While the right to exercise control over the reproductive process of one's body should be enjoyed by every woman, problems will inevitably result from the tendency to tie the technology of birth control to the overall influence of capitalism. Not long ago, condoms were promoted by television commercials—the very same commercials that offer a plethora of capitalist-promoted commodities to the Egyptian public, the overwhelming majority of whom, of course, cannot afford them. Protests resulted in the cancelation of the television commercials, but there are still billboards all around Cairo advertising "Tops" condoms. One afternoon, as I drove through one of the commercial sections of Cairo, I saw such a billboard adjacent to an advertisement for the film *The Seven-Year Itch*, which depicted Marilyn Monroe in her trademark strapless attire. And although abortions are illegal in Egypt, they are apparently surrounded by far less controversy than in the United States. In fact, Shahira Mehrez told me that many women will not hesitate to tell you how many abortions they have had, but will never admit to having a lover.

That enormous numbers of women are compelled to live under male tutelage, so terribly slow in giving way to change, is revealed by the increasing popularity of the veil. Most of the women with whom I spoke—all except a few of whom had chosen not to wear the veil—volunteered observations on the dramatic increase in the number of veiled women in recent years. The veil, of course, has long been considered a symbol of the oppression of women in Islamic culture, and it is frequently assumed that because of it, sexism is qualitatively more injurious for Muslim women than for their Western counterparts. The fixation on the veil among Western scholars—like the contemporary myopic focus on female circumcision—has often distorted attempts to analyze the condition of women in Arab countries. As Irene Gendzier pointed out in her foreword to the American edition of *The Hidden Face of Eve*:

> Wearing the veil, the much-emphasized symbol that has become a substitute for the analysis of women's work and status, is often associated with the petty bourgeois urban sector. Peasants do not practice seclusion, and the use of the veil is an obvious impediment to certain aspects of their work, notably as agricultural producers.[5]

Nawal El Saadawi herself, in discussing the history of the women's movement in Egypt, points out that the leaders of the first Egyptian women's organization, founded by Hoda Shaarawi in 1923, did not really grasp the class character of the veil. Thus, in concentrating their energies on the campaign to eliminate the veil—to the exclusion of issues directly related to the conditions of working women—they managed to further widen the gap between them and their sisters of the poorer classes.

> One of the demonstrations organized by working women ended in a gathering at the premises of the new Women's Federation, but the aristocratic leaders, who were responsible for its activities, paid no attention to the grievances of these poor women, and concentrated on the issue of abolishing the veil, which was unlikely to evoke much enthusiasm amongst them, since in any case the working women in factories and fields had never known what it was to wear a veil.[6]

While it would be a misconception of the nature of Muslim women's oppression to attempt to equate it simplistically with the veil, the prevalence of the veil in urban areas functions nonetheless, I think, as a metaphor for the ideological representation of women, which is imposed—even in contradiction to the realities of their lives—on those who have never been secluded behind the veil. In the words of Fatna Sabbah:

> [T]he veil has a very precise meaning: it represents the denial of the economic dimension of women, who, according to

the tenets of Muslim orthodoxy, are exclusively sexual beings.[7]

The traditional veil, covering most of the woman's face, is worn only by a small minority. Yet the modern veil, which reveals the face but covers all of the hair and sometimes drapes around the chest, is very much in evidence. Although I was aware of the recent resurgence of the veil, I was truly astonished by the sight of so many women in the streets of Cairo attired in various versions of this headpiece.

The majority of women in the Parliament's People's Assembly are veiled, I was told, as are a large portion of young women studying at the university. On several occasions, I spent time with a group of students, all of whom were unveiled. During an automobile trip to Mansoura, several hours outside Cairo, I had the opportunity to hear their feelings about the veil. We drove in a three-car caravan, and at one point or another I rode in each of the three automobiles. I hoped that this might prove to be one of the most provocative discussions of my stay—this was the only time the schedule permitted it—but I felt frustrated as we talked, my eyes continuously drawn to sights along the way. The road followed the tortuous route of the Nile, where unending groups of colorfully dressed women were at work on the riverbank. Not only were they unveiled, but their dresses were frequently pulled up above their knees as they waded in the ancient waters, cleansing their families' vestments for the coming week. These images flew aggressively in the face of the notion that women's bodies are always to be camouflaged so as not to provoke sexual desire in men.

I also saw numerous women working alongside men, picking cotton in the fields and working in the brick-making plants on the side of the road, transporting and stacking the heavy bricks no less efficiently than the men with whom they labored.

One of the young women with whom I spoke during this journey along the Nile wore jeans and sweatshirts each time I saw her. She looked very much like the students I am accustomed to seeing in my classes at San Francisco State University. When I posed a question to her about the relationship between the veil and social perceptions of women's sexuality, she said that men generally seek women whose sexual conduct is precisely the opposite of their own.

> The veiled woman covers herself and is guaranteed to be of good morals. This creates a problem for me, because I have to prove that I am as good as she is. I have to prove that I am not a bad girl, that I don't go around with men, and that I can be interested in serious things.

I asked her why she had decided against wearing the veil, and she hastened to point out that her reason for rejecting the Islamic head covering was quite unique. "Maybe I am only one out of ten or one out of a hundred girls who does not wear the veil because I do not believe in God." This explanation took me by surprise, because I had previously been warned that of all the prevailing taboos, the one surrounding religious belief was respected by virtually everyone. However much one might be prepared to criticize the Islamic fundamentalists, one would hardly go so far as to openly express doubts about the existence of God. Of all the women I encountered in meetings, interviews, and informal conversations, she was the only one who proclaimed herself an atheist. Her friend Randa presented a different side—she said that to interpret the veil simply as a visible mark of adherence to the tenets of Islam was bound to be misleading.

> The veil now doesn't mean anything but the norm. It's the majority who are wearing the veil. If you wear the veil, you have no problems. Before, it was the other way around. The veil was the challenge. My aunt was one of the first girls who wore the veil, and everyone was against it, even her mother, who was quite religious. But now it is the other way around. I decided not to wear the veil because I believe that to be religious is to do everything that the religion says. It is not how I dress but rather how I behave.

Abir, a recent sociology graduate, argued that it should not be assumed that the veil possesses an unambiguous religious significance.

> It is a societal question, not only a religious question. It is the only thing you can cling to during turbulent conditions. It is something solid for some people.

Her friend Naula argued that the veil calls attention to women's readiness to consider themselves sexual objects for men.

> In this day and age, it is not an expression of religion. It is an expression of being ashamed of your body. How can women consider that they are not sexual objects if they cover their hair, their arms, and their legs? The body is still there, the contours are still there. A man who wants to enjoy a

woman's body will still enjoy it whether or not she is wearing a chador. . . . The veiled women still have men walking behind them in the streets making comments.

But Abir spiritedly disagreed.

If you saw the expression on a man's face looking at a woman's behind who is wearing a short, tight skirt, you would really envy a veiled woman. It's terrible the way that men now look at women's bodies.

Indeed, Naula recalled a situation in which she confessed that she was made to feel utterly embarrassed by a veiled woman.

I remember once we were standing in front of the university and it was a particularly hot summer day. This girl passed by us. She was not wearing the veil around the face, but the one that covers the face. She was also wearing gloves. Actually, she was totally covered except for her eyes. Someone in our group remarked that it must be unimaginably hot for her. After she walked a few steps, she turned around and said, "It's hot here now, so you can imagine what it must be like in hell." Her tone was so self-righteous that it made us feel this small.

It was suggested that the veil was occasionally adopted as a matter of expediency. As one of the students said, "Sometimes the veil is a practical convenience. It is not just a symbol of retardation. If a girl wants to go out to work or to study, it is much more convenient." A young woman who cannot afford to spend a great deal of money on clothes or who cannot afford to go to the hairdresser may choose to wear the veil for these secondary economic reasons.

Sheriff Hetata had told me that I might have the opportunity to meet several veiled young women who were members of the women's activist organization Bint Alard—Daughters of the Earth—in Mansoura. The last time he and Nawal El Saadawi had visited Mansoura, several members of the group still wore the veil, although most who join abandon it. But this time all of the women attending the gatherings in Mansoura were unveiled. I did, however, have a brief encounter with a number of veiled women at the Ains Shames University in Cairo, where Mona Aboussena is a professor of English Literature. During the trip to Mansoura, she had jokingly said, "Sometimes I feel ashamed being unveiled—because so many of my students wear the veil." It was she who pulled together a brief informal discussion with some of her students after I delivered a lecture there on education and the struggle for Afro-American equality.

As an outsider, I felt I should proceed as cautiously as possible, so I was careful not to begin by blurting out a question on the significance of the veil. Initially, I asked a woman who wore one of the more austere versions of the veil whether she planned to teach after receiving her degree in English Literature. "No," she answered, in halting though meticulously correct English. "I'm going to stay at home. I'm going to read literature at home." An abbreviated discussion on women and work ensued, the women with veils generally asserting that they did not want to work outside the home. Just as this discussion began to take on the character of an animated argument between the unveiled women, who considered work quite important for themselves, and their veiled counterparts, Mona asked the woman to whom I had first spoken in a rather point-blank manner why she had donned the veil. The young woman, her long-sleeved blue dress covering the entire length of her legs, her white headpiece falling around her shoulders, answered matter-of-factly, "It is in accordance with my religious beliefs." She had first adopted the veil upon reaching puberty.

"Who convinced you to wear it?" Mona asked. "Your parents, the radio . . . ?"

"My reading of the Koran," she responded. "That was enough for me." She went on to explain that "the veil is an order from God. We must obey God in all his orders without any refusals." Throughout the entire meeting, this young woman clutched a small Koran in her hands.

When I later spoke to Nawal El Saadawi in New York, she harshly criticized those who attempt to justify the rising popularity of the veil by representing it as a symbol of resistance to the invasion of Western influences. There is an uncamouflaged message in the popular television programs during which El Sheik Shaarawi praises the veiling of women as an emphatic challenge to the imposition of Western values, followed by a commercial depicting a swimsuit-clad woman advertising a shampoo made in the USA. When Nawal El Saadawi lectures in the United States, she invariably feels compelled to criticize Elizabeth Fernea's film *The Veiled Revolution*, which represents the veil as a positive step on the road to liberation. The film argues that Egyptian women made a profound mistake when they took off the veil at the beginning of this century. Now, they have embraced authentic Arab culture and are thus capable of moving forward on their own terms, rather than on the terms established by Western capitalism. This is an erroneous, apologetic position, according to Nawal El Saadawi. The veil does not represent the authentic culture of her people—and indeed, in *The Hidden Face of Eve*, she offers a historical analysis of the veil as a product of the Judeo-Christian tradition—but rather is, in its contemporary expression, a direct result of prevailing socioeconomic conditions in Egypt.

As unemployment began to rise as a consequence of Sadat's open-door policy, so began the resurrection of the veil. Veiled women were removed from the job market at a time when domestic production was declining in response to the saturation of the market with imported goods from the capitalist countries. Rather than functioning as a means of resisting the invasion of Western capitalist values, the veil serves to consolidate and confirm them by strengthening the sexist social attitudes that facilitate neocolonial economic fetters in Egypt.

Dr. Hoda Badran, a professor in the School of Social Work at the University of Cairo, described the problem in this way:

> The economic system in Egypt, because it is tied to the West, and in particular to United States capitalism, is hindered from being productive. Egypt is being transformed into a consumer society. It is not productive, and it does not generate jobs. In a situation where you don't have jobs, there is competition . . . and people try to find scapegoats . . . That is why there is more prejudice against women than before . . . Also, in a country which has been transformed into a consumer society, it is easy, through the mass media, to use women as sex objects. At the same time, as Awatef Abdel Rahman's study of women and the mass media in Egypt

confirmed, both the print and electronic media almost exclusively present women in the traditional roles of wife and mother.

In a meeting with women writers and artists, the well-known playwright Fathia al Assal argued that Egyptian women should seriously examine problems revolving around sex, if only to understand that the seeming over-emphasis on sexual liberation, which originates in the West, is directly related to the call for women's return to the home—and thus to the donning of the veil. When Nawal El Saadawi said that "women in the West wear nudity the way Arab women wear the veil," I recalled Fathia al Assal's observation. A widely publicized proposal, in fact, calls for working women to be paid half a salary for returning home, thus confining themselves to their mothering, housekeeping, and sexual roles. The playwright asserted that if women permit themselves to become preoccupied with the isolated question of sexual liberation, they might indeed lose sight of the larger issues involved in women's emancipation and those related to the overall national liberation of their people. Having made this point, however, she went on to say that Egyptian women should not be afraid to discuss sexuality. After all, she argued, if one examines the historical development of human societies, it becomes clear that private property emerged at the moment when women became the sexual property of their husbands. Just as the advent of sexual oppression of women coincided with the advent of oppression of social classes, in order for women's bodies to be fully liberated, the social system responsible for that oppression must be eliminated.

Fathia al Assal dramatically illustrated the degree to which the cumulative frustrations of women who have been held captive as sexual property can dangerously erupt by describing a widely publicized criminal case involving a woman who had recently been accused of murdering her husband. After twenty-two years of marriage, this woman was charged with killing her husband and cutting his body into twenty-two pieces, first carving out his eyes, then severing his penis from his body. If newspaper accounts are true, after killing him, she began to pour out all the grievances about which she had remained silent for twenty-two long years. In directing her rage toward her husband's eyes and his sexual organ, she was perhaps symbolically attempting to annihilate the means by which women are transformed into sexual objects. If, indeed, she did kill her husband, she did not even succeed in scratching the surface, for the true culprit is the underlying social system, of which her husband was unfortunately also a victim.

I was extremely impressed by Fathia al Assal's presentation in the meeting, and felt quite excited when she agreed to talk to me in a more informal setting. After the tumultuous discussions at the Hoda Shaarawi Association, we met at Shahira Mehrez's flat and, with Shahira graciously acting as interpreter, we talked late into the night. I did not know at the time that Fathia has the distinction of being one of the first woman playwrights in the Arab world, but I had sensed a courageous and iconoclastic spirit in her presence. Fathia al Assal comes from a family that rapidly acquired wealth in the aftermath of World War II. Her father was married twenty times, and while he made a special effort to educate all his sons, he did not consider knowledge to be an asset in the case of his daughters. Her family moved to Cairo when she was quite young, and although she attended school for a while, her family withdrew her at age nine because of an early puberty. By the time she was fourteen, she began to receive marriage proposals and, after being engaged twice, she married at sixteen. Fathia's interest in progressive political causes had already been aroused by this time, and she told me that an important factor in her husband's attractiveness to her was his political activism. He had spent two years in prison during the 1950's, and in 1981 she herself was detained by Sadat.

Fathia al Assal's career has not been without its difficulties. In fact, Sadat himself was responsible for having her fired after she wrote a serial about a shyster lawyer that was scheduled to be aired on television. The lawyer in the serial was romantically involved with a young woman, who discovered and exposed his fraudulent activities. Sadat assumed that he himself was the underlying inspiration for this character, and he saw to it that Fathia was barred from writing television scripts for two years. When she returned to television, she wrote scripts sharply focused on the predicament of women in Egypt. Modeled on American soap operas, serials on Egyptian television generally explore the lives and loves of the middle and upper classes. Fathia al Assal, however, decided to create women characters who could serve as popular models for resistance to the traditional behavior of women in family relationships. *She and the Impossible*, for example, revolves around an illiterate woman chosen by a landowner as his bride so that she might care for his mother while he studies in Cairo. Upon his return, he informs her that he no longer wants to remain with an ignorant woman. Refusing to divulge to him that she has become pregnant, she leaves unprotestingly and decides to study, work, and bring up her son alone. Twelve years pass before the husband discovers that he has a son. When he proposes that they resume their marriage, she refuses, saying, "The woman you married is not the same as the woman I am today." Moreover, she continues, "My son is a child of circumstances, and I will not come back to you." Initially, the censors categorically rejected this script, insisting that the woman return to her husband for the sake of the child. Five years passed before the program was actually produced and aired in its original form.

In another of her serials, *Moment of Decision*, the leading character is divorced by her husband after twenty years of marriage, when he decides to take another wife. Instead of remaining economically dependent on her former husband, as most divorced women do, she takes a job in a library. Seeking to escape the emptiness of her new solitary life, she begins to read library books, and in the process not only becomes a literate woman, but is inspired to write an autobiographical account of her life. When her book wins an important literary prize, her husband attempts to return. But like the younger woman in the previous serial, she does not give in to his wishes. In the meantime, she has fallen in love with someone else—and as the serial concludes, she faces the man she loves, pressing her prize to her bosom.

I could have spent many more hours listening to Fathia al Assal describe her work, which she did in the manner of the ancient storyteller. Her commitment to the cause of women's freedom permeated every word of her narration. Her most fascinating story summarized the plot of her play *Women without Masks*, which she described as a synthesis of all the women she has ever known. A play that explores the truth of women's condition, it is dedicated to "my friend and daughter, one among a generation to come in a free society yet to be realized. I didn't inherit my mother's bonds and I hope you don't inherit mine." The main character is a woman writer who initially fears the consequences of this truth. As she visualizes what she wants to write, a ballet evokes the historical period of humankind when men and women were equals.

> But the woman is unable to face the beast on an equal basis with the man, and he directs her to the cave where she gives birth. Afterwards he forbids her to leave the cave. The playwright then announces that she wishes to express the condition of this woman when she entered the cave.

A circumcision is performed on stage, and out of an enormous womb, four women are born—a single woman, a married woman, a divorcee, and a widow. By the end of the first act, the playwright has rendered the stories of the four women. However, she has not told the entire truth, and the characters harass her until she confesses:

> In the past we were symbols of life. Our children were named after us. The moment of creation was the moment of love and the moment of love had no other end. Then the whole world was fenced in and we were fenced in with it and named after those who could own land. We were separated from our children and they were named after the master. We were dethroned and our entire history was falsified. We became simply a woman that reproduces. We became a factory that reproduces human beings. One night I woke up and they took me, my hands tied together, like an animal to be slaughtered. "What are they going to do?" I asked my mother. "They are going to butcher you as they have butchered my mother and my mother's mother." I screamed, but the knife

butchered me. My blood was running red before my eyes.
I became two people, one bleeding and the other on the edge
of the knife. "Now you are ready for marriage to a man,"
said my mother. "Now I am half a human being. Who needs
a man unless he is half a human being? I am a body without
feeling. Who needs a body unless he is a body without feeling?" Men shout: "You were circumcised."

When the writer's characters ask her why she had not told
the truth, she answers that she was terrorized. One of the
characters responds, "If you are afraid to tell the truth, you
don't deserve to be a writer." The writer then proceeds to
tell the truth about each of the four women.

As Fathia al Assal would certainly acknowledge, the
speaking of the truth is only the first step in a protracted
process of challenging the forces responsible for the oppression of women. The battle for women's equality in Egypt,
as throughout the Third World and in capitalist countries
as well, must be waged on many fronts. It must target
specific areas, such as the disproportionate burden of poverty shared by women, employment discrimination, illiteracy, inadequate health care, genital mutilation, the
Personal Status Law, and the distorted images of women in
the media. As the campaign against sexist discrimination
must be waged in the political arena, I was particularly
interested in meeting with representatives of the major political parties in Egypt. At various times during my stay in
Cairo, I engaged in discussions with prominent women in
the National Democratic party (Tagamo), the Socialist Labor party, and the New Wafd party.

Fathia al Assal is a member of the Tagamo, which is a
coalition of Marxists, Nasserites, and people of various pro-

gressive political orientations. According to this party's analysis, there has been a significant regression in the status of women since the end of Nasser's era. While the Revolution of 1952 accorded Egypt a leadership position in the national-liberation movement in the Arab world, and while the noncapitalist economic path resulted in a visible amelioration in the economic status of women, important areas were left unchanged. Amina Shafix, the chairperson of the Women's Federation of the Tagamo, pointed out that even under Nasser, no attempt was made to bring women into an independent mass democratic organization—just as there were no independent peasant or youth federations. When Sadat came to power after Nasser's death, it was thus easier to reverse Egypt's previous progressive path.

> He declared the open-door policy, our noncommitment to the national liberation movements and the nonaligned forces (by entering into the Camp David Accords) . . . The old problems of the 1960's helped him in implementing these policies.

Women were directly affected as they found doors closing on job and educational opportunities. Women in the peasant and working classes began to feel the effects of the immigration of labor to the Gulf countries. Sexual crimes became more prevalent, and as a direct result of the socioeconomic crisis, Islamic fundamentalism began to become increasingly influential.

Because women's destiny is tied to the larger political situation, they certainly have a stake in the development of a strong political opposition. And indeed many of the women I met were militant activists, a good number of them having suffered repeated arrests and imprisonments. At an informal gathering of the National Culture Defense Committee, every single woman in the room attested to having been arrested at one time or another. Just a few days prior to this meeting, in fact, several women had been arrested as they peacefully demonstrated against the presence of Israeli representatives at the International Book Fair. Two members of the committee, Dr. Awatef Abdel Rahman and Dr. Latifa Zayat, had personally received letters from Meir Kahane containing uncamouflaged threats on their lives. The Mubarak government had done absolutely nothing in response. Moreover, preparations were under way for an important trial of thirty leading political activists, trade unionists, and working-class peasant and youth leaders. It is known as the case of the Egyptian Communist party, and among the accused is the progressive journalist Farida al Naquash.

Just as I felt I was beginning to understand some of the basic features in the complex structure of oppression affecting women in Egypt, it was time to return home. I was impressed by the strong commitment of so many of the women I met to global struggles for peace and for the New International Economic Order. And I brought home nourishing memories of a brief encounter with Palestinian women living in Cairo, who were justifiably concerned that the issues of Zionism and apartheid remain on the agenda of the upcoming international women's gathering in Nairobi. I realized that Egyptian women faced sexist discrimination, of which some manifestations were not unlike those we face as women in the capitalist countries, and that they were conducting struggles that might benefit from the experiences of women in the socialist countries. But there were also unique issues that women in Egypt would have to work out for themselves. The goal of women's equality in the fullest sense might not be attainable in Egypt's immediate future, but I felt profoundly moved by the invincible determination of so many women to keep the fires of their struggle burning.

NOTES

1. "A Statement on Genital Mutilation" by the Association of African Women for Research and Development, in Miranda Davies, ed., *Third World, Second Sex* (London: Zed Books Ltd. 1983), pp. 217–18.

2. Nawal El Saadawi, *The Hidden Face of Eve* (London: Zed Books Ltd.), p. 7.

3. Ibid., p. 5.

4. Azziza Hussein, "Recently Approved Amendments to Egypt's Law on Personal Status" in Michael Curtis, ed., *Religion and Politics in the Middle East* (Boulder, Colorado: Westview Press, 1981), p. 128.

5. Saadawi, op cit., p. xi.

6. Ibid., p. 175.

7. Fatna A. Sabbah, *Women in the Muslim Unconscious* (New York: Pergamon Press, 1984), p. 13.

Revolution and Womankind:
On Clara Zetkin's *Selected Writings*

Almost one hundred years ago, Clara Zetkin began to work out many of the central concepts associated with the Marxist analysis of women's oppression, concepts that are as relevant today as they were during her era. Along with Friedrich Engels and August Bebel, she emerged as a pioneering theorist of women's status in capitalist society, and a strategist who illuminated the way toward a social order delivered from the effects of institutionalized oppression of women and male-supremacist ideology. Like her heroic contemporary V. I. Lenin, she sought to understand the special oppression of women by placing it within the larger context of the socioeconomic evolution of humankind and consequently attempted to analyze most of the major events within the history of the class struggle of her era.

—Foreword to the 1984 edition of *Clare Zetkin: Selected Writings*, ed. Philip S. Foner (New York: International Publishers, 1984).

In exploring contemporary social issues, she was hardly a dispassionate observer—indeed, she was a deeply committed activist, a woman who became one of the outstanding Communist leaders in the decades surrounding the Great October Revolution. A central figure in German Social Democracy for many years, she later disassociated herself from the party—as did Rosa Luxemburg and Karl Liebknecht—because of its failure to take a firm stand against World War I as imperialist in character and injurious to the interests of the German workers as well as to the international working class. Clara Zetkin was always a staunch defender of the proletariat. She never failed to rely upon a class approach in her theoretical deliberations as well as in her practical political actions. As her theoretical and practical contributions shed light on her own historical period, they can also assist us today to better comprehend the relationship between the fight for socialism and the struggles against racism, for women's equality, and for peace.

Zetkin's first major analysis of the condition of women in capitalist society was presented in a speech she delivered in 1889 at the Paris International Workers' Congress. Emphasizing the centrality of female labor in her presentation, she argued that "the question of women's emancipation . . . in the final analysis is the question of women's work . . ."[1] Zetkin was in agreement with Engels, who, in examining "the peculiar character of the supremacy of the husband over the wife in the modern family" and "the necessity of creating real social equality between them," concluded that "the first condition for the liberation of the wife is to bring the whole female sex back into public industry."[2] Emphasizing the same point, Lenin would later make the following observation:

The chief task of the working women's movement is to fight for economic and social equality, and not only formal equality, for women. The chief thing is to get women to take part in socially productive labour, to liberate them from "domestic slavery," to free them from their stupefying and humiliating subjugation to the eternal drudgery of the kitchen and the nursery.[3]

In order effectively to validate her claim that women could only achieve their liberation via the path of participation in economic production and by thus achieving economic independence, Clara Zetkin had to challenge the prevailing notion that the entrance of women into the labor force militated against the interests of the proletarians.

The Socialists must know that given the present economic development, women's work outside the home is a necessity, that the natural tendency of women's work is either to reduce the working hours that each individual must render to society or to augment the wealth of society, that it is not women's work per se which in competition with men's work lowers wages, but rather the exploitation of female labor by the capitalists who appropriate it.[4]

On several occasions during her speech, Zetkin emphatically pointed out that women ought not be compelled to bear the blame for a process of exploitation that was the sole responsibility of the capitalist class. If, in fact, the large-scale employment of women had led to a longer rather than shorter workday, and if female labor had been used to bring about a decline in the wages of male workers, the solution did not lie in lending support to the prohibition of female labor but rather in recruiting women workers to struggle alongside their male comrades for the ultimate elimination of the capitalist system of production.

Clara Zetkin's arguments in support of women workers contain a logic that can be effectively employed today in defense of stronger affirmative action programs not only for women, but for the racially and nationally oppressed as well. A weakness in her early analysis (which she later corrected) was her failure to acknowledge the need to fight for special protective provisions for women workers in order to guarantee their ability to labor and struggle on an equal basis with men. Nonetheless, she made an important appeal to the male members of the German Social Democratic Party (SPD) to comprehend what a massive involvement of women workers would mean for the battle for socialism, and she issued a passionate call to women workers to recognize the SPD as the authentic bearer of the women's liberation banner. In other words, the participation of women workers would be as indispensable an element in the battle for socialism as the victory of socialism would be in the struggle for women's emancipation.

The title of a speech Clara Zetkin delivered some years later was "Only in Conjunction with the Proletarian Woman Will Socialism Be Victorious." In this presentation to the 1896 Social Democratic Party Congress at Gotha, she argued that the question of women's equality could not be formulated as a single, homogeneous theory, transcending considerations of social class. Bourgeois feminists today who still insist that their strategies for emancipation, which reflect their own class positions, are also valid for working-class and racially oppressed women, have a great deal to learn from Zetkin's analysis. From one class to another—from the grand bourgeoisie to the middle and petit bourgeoisie to the proletariat—the structure of women's oppression varies significantly. She pointed out, however, that all these classes were creations of capitalism and that only women of particular classes that are associated with the capitalist mode of production had developed a historical need to emancipate themselves.

> It was only the capitalist mode of production which created the societal transformations that brought forth the modern women's question by destroying the old family economic system which provided both livelihood and life's meaning for the great mass of women during the pre-capitalist period.[5]

Here, Zetkin raises the important question of the historical genesis of social consciousness. Although women may have been severely oppressed during the precapitalist era, they had not yet encountered the objective circumstances that permitted them to develop an awareness of their suppression. "The women's question . . . is only present within those classes of society who are themselves the products of the capitalist mode of production." She pointed out that among peasants still possessing a natural economy, there was no systematic consciousness of the need to emancipate the women of that class. But "there is a women's question for the women of the proletariat, the bourgeoisie, the intelligentsia and the Upper Ten Thousand."[6] For the haute bourgeoisie, it was a question of women fighting to "dispose of their property in an independent and free manner,"[7] whereas for the other bourgeois strata, whose women were not already in possession of property, the demand focused on equal professional training and equal access to the respective professions. The passage in which Zetkin described the way that the suppression of women and their conscious drive for liberation manifested itself among the working class is important enough to cite here in its entirety:

> As far as the proletarian woman is concerned, it is capitalism's need to exploit and to search incessantly for a cheap labor force that has created the woman's question . . . She went out into the economic life in order to aid her husband in making a living, but the capitalist mode of production transformed her into an unfair competitor. She wanted to bring prosperity to her family, but instead misery descended upon it. The proletarian woman obtained her own employment because she wanted to create a more sunny and pleasant life for her children, but instead she became almost entirely separated from them. She became an equal of the man as a worker; the machine rendered muscular power superfluous and everywhere women's work showed the same results in production as men's work. And since women constitute a cheap labor force and above all a submissive one . . . the capitalists multiply the possibilities of women's work in industry. As a result of all this, the proletarian woman has achieved her independence. But verily the price was very high and for the moment they have gained very little . . . In former times, the rule of a man over his wife was ameliorated by their personal relationship. Between an employer and his worker, however, exists only a cash nexus.[8]

The primary distinction, as Zetkin saw it, between working-class women's fight for equality and the struggles of their bourgeois sisters, was that the latter pitted themselves against the men of their class, while the women proletarians needed to join together with their husbands, brothers, fathers, and sons in order to wage a common battle against the capitalist class. Moreover, what the bourgeois women perceived as ultimate goals, the proletarian women should have interpreted as weapons in the battle to participate in the class struggle on an equal basis with men. Zetkin developed this notion most systematically in her analysis of the relationship between the woman-suffrage campaign and the struggles of working-class women. This analysis is significant not only because of its important historical value, but also because of the lessons to be gleaned from it with respect to the class nature of such contemporary women's struggles as the campaign for the Equal Rights Amendment in the United States. In a paper read before a 1906 Social Democratic Congress in Mannheim, Zetkin asserted that middle-class women perceived woman suffrage as a natural right to participate in the political processes of an equally natural and immutable bourgeois society. For working-class women, the ballot was, on the contrary, a social right, a demand that had arisen as a clear consequence of the emergence of the capitalist economic system. Moreover:

> The middle class women really wish to obtain this social reform because they think it is a measure which will strengthen and support the whole of middle class society. The working women demand the suffrage not only to defend their economic and moral interests of life, but they wish for it as a help against the oppression of their class by men and they are particularly eager for it in order to aid in the struggle against the capitalist class.[9]

Thus, women's right to vote assumes entirely different dimensions among women of opposing social classes. As Zetkin pointed out in a resolution she introduced during the

International Socialist Congress at Stuttgart in 1907, Socialist women could not place as much weight on suffrage as did bourgeois women because the achievement of the right to vote would not fundamentally affect the underlying cause of women's oppression, i.e., private property. After all, the male proletariat, which was permitted to exercise the franchise, remained nonetheless severely exploited. In other words,

> the granting of suffrage to the female sex does not eliminate the class differences between the exploiters and the exploited from which the most serious obstacles to the free and harmonious development of the female proletarian are derived.[10]

If, however, woman suffrage emerged as a significant demand in working-class women's battles, it was because the ballot was potentially a powerful weapon to be wielded in the larger class struggle against capitalism. In fact, it was a weapon required not only by female workers, but by their class brothers as well. As increasing numbers of women entered the ranks of labor, becoming integral members of the working class, the fight for woman suffrage would increasingly become "a struggle for the capture of political power by the proletariat."[11]

Considering the recent defeat of the Equal Rights Amendment in the United States and the escalation of anti-ERA propaganda by organized right-wing forces, the protracted nature of the struggle may well be comparable to the long fight for woman suffrage. What Clara Zetkin said about the campaign to extend the ballot to women might well be said today about the ERA campaign:

We know that we shall not obtain the victory of woman suffrage in a short time, but we know, too, that in our struggles for this measure we shall revolutionise hundreds of thousands of minds. We carry on our war, not as a fight between the sexes, but as a battle against the political might of the possessing classes; as a fight which we carry on with all our might and main without hatred of the other sex; a fight whose final aim and whose glory will be that (one day) the proletariat in its entirety, without distinction of sex, shall be able to call out to the capitalist order of society, "You rest on us, you oppress us, and, see, how the building which you have erected is tottering to the ground."[12]

Clara Zetkin emphasized again and again that the larger historical context of the battle for women's liberation was the working-class drive for socialism. A contemporary feminist theorist with distinct anti-Communist leanings writes that

ever since the existing socialist societies dawned on this earth disillusionment with socialism, which results from revolution, has been an impetus to the emergence of feminist theory.[13]

Had she, like Clara Zetkin, more seriously examined the real relationship between socialism and the women's movement, she would have realized that the birth of socialism, since the triumph of the October Revolution, has served as an inspiration and a beacon to countless working women across the globe. When the face of history was transformed by the Russian Revolution, Zetkin joined millions of workers throughout the world in enthusiastically greeting this triumph.

> The Bolsheviks have reached their goal in a bold assault which has no parallel in history. Governmental power is in the hands of the Soviets. What has transpired is the revolutionary dictatorship of the proletariat.[14]

When she wrote about the impact of the revolution on the Muslim women of the former colonies of czarist Russia, her observations could be applied, many years later, to the situation in the United States with respect to the struggles waged by Black working-class and other racially and nationally oppressed women. The active strivings of Moslem women for their freedom

> confirm the fact that the proletarian revolution will indeed turn out to be a world revolution in which even the last suppressed and enslaved individual will free himself by his own strength.[15]

Implied in Zetkin's discussion of the liberation struggle among Muslim women is a message that is clearly relevant to the women's movement today. Working-class and racially oppressed women confront sexist oppression in a way that reflects the real and complex objective interconnections between class exploitation, racist oppression, and male supremacy. Whereas a white middle-class woman's experience of sexism incorporates a relatively isolated form of this oppression, working-class women's experiences necessarily place sexism in its context of class exploitation, and Black women's experiences further incorporate the social factor of racism. These are by no means subjective experiences; rather, there is an objective interrelationship between racism and sexism in that the general context of both forms of oppression in our time is the class struggle unfolding between monopoly capitalism and the working class.

It is of special importance to the progressive people in the United States who understand the extent to which racism is interwoven in the history of this country and the extent to which it has been used as a tool to set asunder the unity of the working class, to recognize that Clara Zetkin played an indispensable role in the extension of international solidarity to the struggle for Black equality in the United States. As the head of the International Red Help, she appealed in 1932 to progressive people throughout the world to defend the nine Scottsboro youths who had been fraudulently convicted of raping two white women in a small town in Alabama. She specifically called upon the international movement to prevent the executions of the eight who had been sentenced to death. Of course, the struggle against the death penalty—and especially as it focuses on the racist implication of capital punishment—is very much alive fifty years after Clara Zetkin summoned forth support for the Scottsboro Nine. In 1988, approximately two thousand people are on death row in the United States, and almost half of them are Blacks and other people of color.

Before anything else, Clara Zetkin was a woman of peace. While she never capitulated in the midst of the battles of the working class, she consistently emphasized the importance of the struggle for peace as a factor in the class struggle itself.

> Imperialist wars are directed against the workers; they are the inevitable expression of the very being of capitalism. The

first decisive step toward demolishing the system of blood-sucking capitalism must be strong and inexorable recognition that the workers are against imperialist wars.[16]

Indeed, the efforts to counter monopoly capitalism's stronghold in those countries that have not yet joined hands for peace with the Soviet Union and the socialist community of nations are inherently tied to the struggle to end the threat of nuclear annihilation, which looms over us all. Peace among nations, as Clara Zetkin repeatedly insisted, is always in the interests of the working class.

NOTES

1. Clara Zetkin, *Selected Writings* (New York: International Publishers, 1984), p. 45.

2. Frederick Engels, *The Origin of the Family, Private Property and the State* (New York: International Publishers, 1970), pp. 137–38.

3. V. I. Lenin, *The Emancipation of Women* (New York: International Publishers, 1966), p. 81.

4. Clara Zetkin, *Selected Writings* (New York: International Publishers, 1984), p. 45.

5. Ibid., p. 72.

6. Ibid., p. 74.

7. Ibid.

8. Ibid., pp. 76–77.

9. "Social Democracy and Woman Suffrage," a paper read by Clara Zetkin to the Conference of Women belonging to the Social Democratic Party held at Mannheim before the opening of the 1906 Annual Congress of German Social-Democracy. Pamphlet published by the Twentieth Century Press Ltd. London: 1907, p. 7.

10. Ibid., p. 99.

11. Clara Zetkin, *Social Democracy and Woman Suffrage*, p. 15.

12. Ibid., p. 16.

13. Batya Weinbaum, *The Curious Courtship of Women's Liberation &
Socialism* (Boston: South End Press), 1978, p. 7.

14. Zetkin, *Selected Writings*, p. 138.

15. Ibid., p. 158.

16. Clara Zetkin, *The Toilers Against War* (New York: Workers Library
Publishers, 1934), p. 73.

ON
EDUCATION
AND CULTURE

Imagining the Future

I want to thank you graduating seniors for inviting me on this momentous occasion to share with you some of my own political experiences, and to offer you my ideas on the opportunities and challenges that await you. I must confess, however, that I was quite surprised to learn that you had chosen me to be your commencement speaker. I realize now that I had developed preconceptions about the youth of today based on propagandistic notions that the younger generation, by and large, is unconcerned and apolitical—and perhaps more interested in MTV than in anything else. However, unconcerned and apolitical young people obviously would not have invited a woman who is a Communist and activist in radical political struggles to address their graduating class. I definitely owe you an apology.

My generation is remembered for the militant activism of the sixties and early seventies. We had good cause to

---

—Originally presented as a commencement address to the Berkeley High School graduating class, June 16, 1983.

involve ourselves in those struggles: the southern states were still brutally segregated; Black people risked their lives to exercise their voting rights; there were no Black, Latino, or Asian Studies programs in the universities or the high schools. Ronald Reagan was elected governor of California and was responsible for, among other things, charging me with three capital crimes—murder, kidnapping, and conspiracy—as well as placing me on the FBI's ten most wanted criminals list. Richard Nixon was elected president of the country, and showed his true colors by conducting a bloody war of aggression against the people of Vietnam. He further orchestrated a smaller-scale domestic war of political repression against the Black Panther party and other Black activist organizations.

We had good cause to align ourselves with radical mass movements during that period. We spun dreams of a better world—one without racism, without economic injustices, without war. We imagined a more humane future, but we also risked our very lives to defeat racism and U.S. military aggression against Southeast Asia.

Now, it is your turn to imagine a more humane future—a future of justice, equality, and peace. And if you wish to fulfill your dreams, which remain the dreams of my generation as well, you must also stand up and speak out against war, against joblessness, and against racism.

Your generation is growing to maturity during a time of great danger—danger that is exemplified by U.S. aggression in El Salvador and Nicaragua and U.S. collusion with South Africa's apartheid government. The young men graduating in this class are among those who would be drafted in the event of a military mobilization aimed at any one of those countries.

But there is an even greater danger. The United States now possesses approximately one thousand nuclear warheads, which are literally capable of consuming the entire world in atomic flames. This is bad enough as it is—but think about the man whose finger is on the nuclear trigger. You are not old enough to remember Ronald Reagan during his heyday in Hollywood. Those were the days of *Bedtime for Bonzo* (his chimpanzee co-star); those were his Death Valley days. Now many of us fear that Reagan might play with an MX missile as he once played with Bonzo—or that he might decide one day to lead us all back to Death Valley.

Yesterday's paper contained an ironic photograph of your president sitting in front of a class of high-school seniors. Perhaps he needs to take a seat among them instead of sitting in front of them. In any event, it seems to me that some of you graduating seniors would probably be far more capable of running this country than the man who is currently pretending to do so. I seriously doubt whether any of you would be so quick to lead the entire world in the direction of global nuclear destruction.

Many of the young men graduating this afternoon will soon be—if they haven't already been—called upon to register for the draft. The draft-registration law is three years old, and it has become a nightmare for hundreds of thousands of young people like yourselves. Over seven hundred thousand of them have, at the risk of imprisonment, already refused to comply with the draft law. Attempts have even been made by the federal government to railroad students into registering by threatening to cut off their financial aid.

In the lyrics of your theme song, John Lennon says, "Imagine all the people living together in peace." But we must be more specific: "Imagine no MX missiles, no cruise missiles, no Pershing II missiles." We must also do more than imagine. We must march, protest, petition, and pursue whatever other avenues of collective resistance will guarantee that one day all people will live together in total peace, free of the threat of nuclear destruction. Today's youth is tomorrow's hope. It is therefore incumbent upon all of you to work so that you and future generations can "be all that you can be"—but certainly not in the army, navy, air force, or marines.

> Imagine no possession
> I wonder if you can
> No need for greed or hunger
> or brotherhood of man.

Today, of course, the world does not really belong to its inhabitants. There are those—a minute segment of the population—who have usurped most of the wealth in the capitalist world and there are others—the vast majority—who have comparatively little. Many in this majority don't even have enough to survive. Entire families are walking the streets today with no homes, no jobs, no guarantee that they will have food for their next meal.

Joblessness is a special problem for young people, particularly young Black people and others from racially oppressed communities. It is a problem for young women, especially young women of color. How many of you have ever imagined that after graduation there would be a well-paying, creative job awaiting you—or that a scholarship might enable you to attend college? Quite a few of you, no doubt. But you are dealing with a government that cares nothing about its young people and their future. The Reagan administration is the most brutally antiyouth administration in the entire history of our country. There have been massive cuts in most of the programs that were of any benefit to the young—job training, summer-job programs, health, education, counseling, and recreational programs. The funds for these programs have been transferred to the military. Right here in Berkeley, a Youth Employment Program was established by your current mayor, the Honorable Gus Newport, which united the school district, the private sector, and city government. But Reagan's interference has caused the program to dwindle to a mere shadow of what it was before.

Reagan's preposterous solution to the problem of youth unemployment is the subminimum wage or the so-called "summer wage." Originally, he had proposed a $1.57 minimum wage for all teenagers. Who would want to work for what amounts to slave wages? He later modified it to a $2.50 minimum wage for summer work. Think of the millions of dollars companies like McDonald's might make under such conditions. They are already thriving on cheap teenage labor. Young people should not only earn the minimum wage, the minimum wage itself ought to be doubled! Moreover, an immediate training program should be implemented as a prerequisite for the creation of 5 million jobs for young people in a public-works project to rebuild the nation's cities.

Imagine a shorter work week—thirty hours instead of forty—with no cut in pay. This would create millions of new jobs for young people.

Imagine that all the colleges and universities in the country could be mobilized in order to educate all of our young people for the future—for free.

Imagine that in jobs and in the universities, there would be strong affirmative-action measures so that Black, Asian, Latino, Pacific Island, and Native American youth might finally overcome the stifling legacy of racism. Imagine that young women had exactly the same opportunities as young men.

Imagine, indeed, a world without sexism. Imagine a world without homophobia.

Imagine that we lived in a world without racism.

Imagine that the Ku Klux Klan had already been relegated to the distant past and that we would never again have to worry about the establishment of camps where young white kids learn to hate and brutalize Black people, Mexican-Americans, Native Americans, and Jews.

Imagine that we lived in a world where a five-year-old Black child named Patrick Mason could not be callously murdered by a white police officer in Stanton, California, who later justified his action by saying that the child had a toy gun in his hands. Imagine that we lived in a country where a young Chinese American named Vincent Chin could not be beaten to death with a baseball bat by two unemployed autoworkers who mistook him for Japanese and decided to vent their anger about Japanese automobile imports by killing "one of them."

Imagine that we lived in a world where Mexicans, Central Americans, and Haitians without immigration papers would not be rounded up like cattle and incarcerated in concentration camps, only to be shipped back to their own countries, where they face abject poverty and brutal political repression.

Imagine that we lived in a world where a young Black

activist named Eddie Carthan, duly elected first Black mayor of Tchula, Mississippi, could not be framed on serious felony charges and sentenced to many years in prison because he wished to improve the conditions of the poor in his town.

Imagine that we lived in a world where physically and mentally disabled youth would not be subjected to devastating routine discrimination.

Imagine that we lived in a world without capital punishment. Today, approximately twelve hundred people languish in death-row cells in the prisons across this land; some of them were mere children when they were sentenced to die. Almost half of them are people of color.

But, my young friends—my young sisters and brothers—we must do more than engage in such flights of imagination. All of us, the young and the old alike, women as well as men, must stand up, speak out, and fight for a better world.

We must not allow another Vietnam to explode in El Salvador. We must prevent the subversion of the revolutions in Nicaragua and Grenada. It is up to you to say, "Hell, no, we won't go . . . hell, no, we won't register for anything except to vote Ronald Reagan out of office . . . hell, yes, we will support Ron Dellums in Congress and Gus Newport, the progressive mayor of our city who has taken militant stands for free, integrated education and jobs for all youth."

And we must say—as Dr. Martin Luther King, Jr., said twenty years ago, "I have a dream." Your generation was not yet born when Dr. King led the earthshaking march on Washington in 1963, but you hold in *your* hands the power to lead this country in a direction that will reflect what you are able to imagine now in your hearts and minds.

Finally, my young friends, remember that you must not only imagine and dream about your future goals—and, indeed, the future of the world—but you must also stand up, unite, and fight for peace, jobs, equality, and freedom!

Reaping Fruit
and Throwing Seed

This graduation ceremony for UCLA's Black students celebrates the collective achievement of an educational goal toward which you have all worked arduously over the last years. At the same time, it reflects the vitality of a legacy forged by the Black liberation movement almost two decades ago. My own struggle here at UCLA, which was a response to then Governor Ronald Reagan's decision to fire me from my faculty position in the philosophy department because of my membership in the Communist party, was one of the many fronts in the defense of Black people's right to participate in the educational process of this university. I therefore feel a close personal connection with you graduating Afro-American students here at UCLA.

Today, though we have hardly achieved our goal of eliminating the racism that pervades the educational institutions of this country and this university in particular (in fact, we have witnessed a process of backsliding over the last years),

—Address to the graduating Black students at UCLA, June 15, 1985.

it is a glorious victory that you as Afro-American students are presently receiving your diplomas from UCLA. You must never forget that people marched and organized, were arrested and lost their jobs—some even lost their lives—in order to clear the way for this victorious moment. I urge you to reflect seriously on your responsibilities to those whose activism made it possible for you to reach this important goal in your lives. As you reap the fruit of past struggles, you must also throw seed for future battles.

As you celebrate these rites of passage, be aware that the masses of our people, especially our youth—your peers— are suffering the effects of increasingly deleterious forms of racist discrimination. The Children's Defense Fund in Washington, D.C., has just published a report entitled *Black and White Children in America: Key Facts*. The report points out that compared to five years ago, Black children today are far more likely to be born into poverty, to have unemployed parents, to be unemployed themselves as teenagers, and they are far *less* likely to go to college after graduation from high school.

Between the late 1960's and the mid-1970's, undoubtedly as a result of the marches, demonstrations, and strikes around the demand that more of our people be accepted into institutions of higher learning, a measurable degree of progress was achieved. As a matter of fact, by 1977, the rate of college attendance was about the same for Black students as for white students. But by 1982—only five years later—white youth were about 45 percent more likely to attend college than their Black counterparts.

The Children's Defense Fund report suggests that this marked deterioration in Black people's access to institutions of higher learning is directly attributable to the increased impoverishment of the Afro-American community. Almost half of all Black children are poor today, while one out of six white children is officially below the poverty level. Black children are five times more likely to be dependent on welfare than white children.

The Reagan administration boasts that its policies have resulted in a significant decline in the rate of unemployment, yet our communities are still suffering depression levels of joblessness. Official statistics of soaring Black unemployment do not even reflect the enormous numbers of Black people who have been unsuccessfully searching for work for so long that, out of despair, they have become inactive job seekers. Untold numbers of our women, lacking education and job skills, are unable to find jobs that will pay even the expenses incurred in the process of working. That is to say, single mothers frequently cannot earn enough to pay for child care, transportation, clothing, etc.—not to speak of rent, food, and the remaining basic necessities. Consequently, they are often compelled to apply for Aid to Families with Dependent Children (AFDC), simply because they cannot afford to work.

However, education alone is not the cure for these symptoms we suffer as a result of the racist epidemic that infects our government and our society. Regardless of their educational levels, Afro-American women and men are less likely to be employed today than their white counterparts. Unemployment is three times higher among Black male college graduates than among white male college graduates. It is indeed scandalous that young Black college graduates today have an unemployment rate almost as high as that of white high-school dropouts. About one out of every four Black college graduates is unable to find a job.

Those of you who are fortunate enough to find work will discover that your earnings are likely to be shockingly less than those of your white counterparts. In 1982, among college graduates, white males earned a median annual income of twenty-nine thousand dollars, as compared to Black males, who earned nineteen thousand dollars. White women earned eighteen thousand dollars, while Black women earned a mere sixteen thousand dollars—thirteen thousand dollars less than white men.

This, my young sisters and brothers, is what awaits you. Even though you are among the most privileged of our people, reaping the fruits of decades of sacrifice and struggle by our communities, your futures are far from secure.

What is the political context of this crisis afflicting the Afro-American community? It is the Reagan administration's all-out attack on the labor movement and the attendant official efforts to reverse the most important gains of the civil rights movement. The U.S. Civil Rights Commission has been virtually dismantled, considering that Clarence Pendleton, Reagan's Black yes-man, is leading it in a direction that will render it a rubber-stamp agency for the administration's racist policies, rather than the watchdog for civil rights that it was conceived to be.

The general offensive against the working class means that the economic conditions of Black people have rapidly deteriorated. The general assault on women means that conditions of Black women have become especially unbearable. This intensification of racism incited by the Reagan administration involves a violent escalation of police crimes in the Afro-American community. Not very long ago, police in the City of Brotherly Love conducted an attack on a Black household that was unprecedented in its brutality. The siege of the MOVE house in Philadelphia resulted in the murders of eleven Black women, children, and men, and the arson of some sixty homes in the Black community. Not only must the police be held accountable, but the Black mayor—Wilson Goode, himself—must be made to bear responsibility for this warfare against our community.

The administration's racist agenda also has serious international implications. As a direct result of U.S. confederacy with South Africa, under the guise of "constructive engagement"—which more appropriately deserves to be called "destructive engagement"—over four hundred South Africans have been murdered by the police and the military since the new year. Many thousands more have been banned, arrested, imprisoned, and tortured. Freedom fighters and community leaders of the United Democratic Front are facing death sentences. Nelson Mandela has been in prison and Winnie Mandela has been banned or under house arrest for the last twenty-five years.

Here in this country, a vigorous anti-apartheid movement has emerged over the last six months, attracting tens of thousands of participants in picket lines, marches, demonstrations, and rallies. Literally thousands of people have been arrested for engaging in civil disobedience. Longshore workers in San Francisco refused to unload South African cargo, and students throughout the state of California—from UC Berkeley to Santa Cruz to UCLA—have militantly and creatively dramatized their demands that the University of California divest its holdings from companies operating in South Africa. The Regents will be meeting next week, no doubt in an attempt to develop justifications for their refusal to divest. But it should be clear to all of us here today that it is only a matter of time before this university and all American interests in South Africa will be compelled to cease dealing in the blood money euphemistically called corporate profits. The Regents declare apologetically that divestment will cause them to lose money. If this is indeed the case, then it is a small price to pay for the immoral stance of having profited for so long from a situation where Black workers are paid one-tenth the wages of white workers.

In the end, the people of South Africa will prevail. They will be victorious with or without our help. However, what we do in this country can certainly hasten their moment of victory. It is our responsibility not only to continue to fight for divestment, but to press for an end to all trade relations with South Africa. Ultimately, all economic, cultural, and political relations with South Africa must be severed until the edifice of apartheid comes tumbling down.

These are some of the many urgent challenges confronting us today, and indeed you as Afro-American graduates of this institution have a special responsibility to participate in and give leadership to the movements that arise to meet these challenges. You must not only be concerned about Black people in the United States, but about Chicanos, Latinos, Asians, Pacific Islanders, and Native American people. You must also be concerned about the working class as a whole, and you should understand the bonds that tie us all, men as well as women, to the fight for women's equality. You must not only focus on our people's plight in South Africa, for our people are also in Nicaragua, El Salvador, and in the Middle East. Finally, as Afro-American students, you should seize the opportunity to play an instrumental role in the effort to rid this planet of the threat of nuclear omnicide.

On this, the occasion of your college graduation, which

marks the culmination of perhaps more years of your respective lives than any of you as individuals will ever again
dedicate to the attainment of a single personal goal, I urge
you to reflect not only on your own time and efforts, but
on the struggles of your forebears as well, which made it
possible for you to attend this university, to gain an education, and to collect your diplomas here today. You have
reached a point in your lives when it becomes necessary for
you to rededicate your time and efforts to the cause and
struggles that will pave the way for your successors—generations of Afro-Americans to come—that they may live in
a peaceful world free of the threat of nuclear destruction and
that they might one day reflect on the life, the education,
and the future you have offered them.

Ethnic Studies: Global Meanings

The concept of ethnic studies, with its focus on the cultural demands of racially oppressed people in the United States, has always involved, along with its challenge to racism in our own educational system, a bridge-building process inviting us to identify with the struggles and accomplishments of oppressed people of color around the world. While we have recognized the bonds linking us to Africa, Asia, the Carribean, the Middle East, and Latin America as having been wrought by our respective racial and cultural heritages, we must be equally cognizant of the fact that these ties have been enormously strengthened by our common pursuit of dignity and freedom. "What is Africa to me?" W.E.B. DuBois once asked.

> Africa is, of course, my fatherland. Yet neither my father nor my father's father ever saw Africa or knew its meaning or cared for it. My mother's folk were closer and yet their

—Address given at San Francisco State University, April 14, 1984.

direct connection, in culture and race, became tenuous; still my tie to Africa is strong. On this vast continent were born and live a large portion of my ancestors going back a thousand years or more. The mark of their heritage is upon me in color and hair. These are obvious things, but of little meaning in themselves; only important as they stand for real and more subtle differences from other men . . .

But one thing is sure and that is the fact that since the fifteenth century these ancestors of mine and their other descendants have had a common history; have suffered a common disaster and have one long memory . . . [T]he real essence of this kinship is its social heritage of slavery; the discrimination and insult; and this heritage binds together not simply the children of Africa, but extends through . . . Asia and into the South Seas. It is this unity that draws me to Africa.[1]

Indeed, the Afro-American people's centuries-long search for freedom has always borne a special relationship to the national-liberation struggles on the continent of Africa. It is not mere coincidence that 1960, the year of the militant sit-ins throughout the South—which marked a turning point in the civil rights movement—was also called Africa Year, because the colonial empires of Africa suffered decisive blows. Cameroon, Togo, Senegal, Mali, Madagascar, Congo-Kinshasha, Congo-Brazzaville, Somalia, Dahomey, Niger, Upper Volta, the Ivory Coast, Chad, the Central African Republic, Nigeria, Gabon, Mauritania—seventeen states in all proclaimed their independence in 1960.

For the Black, Puerto Rican, and Chicano movements of the 1960's, the Cuban Revolution was also a powerful influence. As we young people organized our communities, marched, and demonstrated to dramatize our opposition to racism, as we battled the brutal repression of the police, we were inspired by the revolutionary heroism of Che Guevara, Fidel Castro, and Haydee Santamaria. We felt strengthened in our beliefs by the knowledge that the outlawing of racial discrimination was among the first acts of the Cuban Revolution. As we explored the implications of Black and Latino cultural consciousness, we felt confirmed by the promotion of the African dimension of Cuban culture in music, dance, and education.

In examining the international influences on Third World struggles in the United States—and particularly those that culminated with the establishment of the institution of ethnic studies—we must not fail to acknowledge the immense impact of the Vietnam War. The heroic people of Vietnam, in their efforts to repel imperialist assaults and forge a new social order, were a continuing inspiration to those of us who were propelled forward by our vision of a new social order in our own country, the dominion of imperialism. As women, we were especially moved by the visible contributions Vietnamese women were making at every level of their people's struggle. Madame Nguyen Thi Binh emerged as the symbol of the process that merged women's emancipation with national liberation. And certainly both the Cuban and Vietnamese experiences allowed increasingly large numbers of political activists in our country seriously to consider socialism as our ultimate strategic goal.

The struggle for ethnic studies in the United States revealed a characteristic centrality of the demand for education within the larger movement for justice and equality. Throughout the evolution of the Afro-American liberation movement, from the era of slavery to the present, the fight for education has been the very heart of the quest for freedom. In the international arena, demands revolving around equality and justice in education have likewise played pivotal and catalytic roles in battles for national liberation. Consider, for example, the case of South Africa. In 1976, between June 16 and August 30, more than sixteen thousand rounds of ammunition were fired by police in an effort to put down the student and worker insurrection in Soweto. This rebellion was triggered by the attempt on the part of the apartheid government to force Africans to study certain subjects in the language of their oppressors, the white Afrikaaners. But it evolved into much more than a challenge to Afrikaans; it became a protest against the entire system of Bantu education, which was designed to train Africans for subordination. As the African National Congress observed at the time:

> It is not just a strike against Afrikaans as a medium of instruction but a political protest by an enslaved, oppressed people against the whole concept of Bantu education.[2]

The ANC's analysis of Bantu education contains numerous parallels to the educational predicament of Black, Latino, Asian, and Native American peoples in this country:

> This education system is an instrument for entrenching white domination. It prepares the African child for the role of an underdog, a supplier of cheap labour who will not identify himself with the aspirations of the oppressed masses for national liberation. It is a role of ensuring the privileged position of the white man, insulating the African child from world events and confining him to the lies and distortions that are prepared by the Boers in order to retard the intellectual de-

velopment of Blacks. The education he is given glorifies tribalism; the child is made to accept the white man as saviour whose divine mission it is to dominate the lives of the Black people and determine how, where and how long each one of them should live. Indeed it is an education for servitude.[3]

During the Soweto uprising, practically all of the offices of the Bantu administration were burned down. Beer halls and liquor stores, which are operated by the apartheid government and are its major source of income in the Black areas, were also targeted. "Less Liquor, Better Education" and "More Schools, Fewer Beer Halls" were the slogans shouted by students and scrawled on walls throughout the township of Soweto.

At the time of the insurrection, the apartheid government boasted that it was spending more money on African education than ever before. But even so, there was and continues to be an increasingly wider gap between white and Black education. In 1964, the government spent ten times as much money on white students as on Black students. By 1974, fifteen times as much money was being spent on white students' education as on that of Black students. As Nelson Mandela said in a message smuggled out of prison, where he has been since 1962:

> [The] verdict is loud and clear: Apartheid has failed. Our people remain unequivocal in its rejection. The young and the old, parent and child, all reject it. At the forefront of the 1976–77 wave of unrest were our students and youth. They come from the universities, high schools and even primary schools . . .
> But after more than twenty years of bantu education the

circle is closed and nothing demonstrates the utter bank-
ruptcy of Apartheid as the revolt of our youth. The evils,
the cruelty and the inhumanity of Apartheid have been there
from its inception. And all Blacks—Africans, Coloreds and
Indians—have opposed it all along the line.[4]

The struggle for education in Grenada has yielded decisive
lessons relevant to the continued defense, expansion, and
deepening of ethnic studies on this campus, in the state, and
throughout the country. We who are associated with the
School of Ethnic Studies here at San Francisco State feel a
special bond with the people of Grenada, for we sponsored
a recent visit of the National Performing Company of Grenada to San Francisco. We were in the process of establishing
an exchange program between our university and the Teachers College of Grenada, which would have been in effect
today if not for the assassination of Prime Minister Maurice
Bishop and the U.S. invasion of Grenada.

The devastating legacy of colonial education was elo-
quently described by the late prime minister:

Perhaps the worst crime that Colonialism left our country,
has indeed left all former colonies, is the education system.
This is so because that system was used to teach our people
an attitude of self-hate, to get them to abandon our history,
our culture, our values. To get them to accept the principles
of white superiority, to destroy our confidence, to stifle our
creativity, to perpetuate in our society class privilege and
class difference. The colonial masters recognized very early
on that if they get a subject people to think like they do, to
forget their own history and their own culture . . . then they
have already won the job of keeping us in perpetual domi-
nation and exploitation.[5]

At the very top of the list of priorities following the triumph of the New Jewel Movement in March of 1979 was the transformation of the educational system inherited from the dictatorship of Eric Gairy. Jacqueline Creft, Minister of Education, Culture, and Women's Affairs until she was assassinated during the bloody coup against the Bishop government, put it this way:

> We were determined to change a system which so powerfully excluded the interests of the mass of our people, and which also wove webs of fear, alienation and irrelevance around our children's minds . . . Whether it was Little Miss Muffet, The Cow Jumped over the Moon, William the Conqueror, Wordsworth's Daffodils or the so-called "discoveries" by Christopher Columbus of the so-called "New World."[6]

Although the revolutionary process in Grenada was abruptly interrupted in the fall of 1983 by the internal coup and the U.S. military invasion, almost five years had been devoted to the creation of a new educational structure that brought literacy, a new cultural identity, and an increasingly complex political consciousness to the masses of people. During that time, billboards bearing slogans such as "Education, A Right Not A Privilege" decorated the entire island. Young teachers enthusiastically taught adults the basic skills of reading and writing, while new schools were established to provide free public education to all.

Textbooks were being rewritten to reflect the history and heritage of the Grenadians. In the earliest primary grades, books had already been published in the people's spoken language, as opposed to the queen's English, thereby facilitating the transition from the spoken to the written language as well as legitimizing the rich oral tradition of Grenada. Culture had begun to flourish during those four and a half years, and important research was being conducted for the very first time into the African roots of the Grenadian experience. On the island of Carriacou, for example, the traditional Big Drum Dance was being reverently taught and studied as one of the most powerful cultural affirmations today of the Grenadian people's African heritage.

"The Grenadian Revolution," Jacqueline Creft declared, "is a revolution in education too."

> It is steeped in the belief that knowledge and economic power must be inseparable and that our people's total liberation can only come with the balance and equal consolidation of both.[7]

This bold and promising experiment in education was violently halted, yet the spirit of that double-faceted revolution lives on. We ought to constantly remind ourselves not only of the importance of studying the Grenadian experience for the purpose of gleaning lessons that are applicable to our own struggles for relevant education, but also of the necessity to support those who still carry forth the legacy of their people's revolution.

If the Grenada Revolution has been temporarily crushed, the Sandinista Revolution in Nicaragua is fortunately still vibrantly marching on. Certainly, the Nicaraguan experience in the realm of education should be carefully studied by all who wish to render the educational process relevant to the historical realities of oppressed people. It is said that Nicaragua itself is a school, for over 40 percent of the population are involved in some capacity in the organized educational process. At the time of Somoza's defeat, however, about half of the population was unable to read and write. In most rural areas, in fact, the illiteracy rate was 75–80 percent, and in some villages there existed a 100 percent illiteracy rate among women. Moreover, in the words of Ernesto Cardenal, minister of culture,

> [l]iterature, theater and song were suppressed. Books were banned . . . That is why we have a literature which is eminently that of protest, a political song, and a popular street theatre which was for agitation, although at times clandestine.[8]

Ironically, Cardenal points out, Tolstoy was banned because he was a Russian author, but because of its title, *The Holy Family* by Marx and Engels was permitted.

Just five weeks after the Sandinista triumph, plans began to take shape for a massive governmental crusade against illiteracy. On March 24, 1980, the literacy campaign was launched, as one hundred thousand volunteers began the process of teaching others to read and write. In order to guarantee the most concentrated and the most extensive action possible, the high schools were shut down for one semester, permitting the students to organize classes in the most remote regions of the country. When this phase of the literacy campaign concluded five months later on August 30, the illiteracy rate had dropped from 52 percent to about 12 percent. This feat is indubitably one of the most remarkable triumphs of the Sandinista Revolution. Poor people in Nicaragua—the peasantry as well as the urban indigent population—had not only learned the alphabet, they had not only learned the mechanics of reading and writing, they had also begun to learn about the economic, political, and social realities surrounding them. In the words of Fernando Cardenal, director of the literacy campaign:

> We believe that in order to create a new nation we must begin with an education that liberates people. Only through knowing their past and their present, only through understanding and analyzing their reality can people choose their future. Education, therefore, must encourage people to take charge of their lives, to learn to become informed and effective decision makers, and to understand their roles as responsible citizens possessing rights and obligations. . . . Education for liberation means people working together to gain an understanding of and control over society's economic, political and social forces in order to guarantee their full participation in the creation of a new nation.[9]

That is what the Nicaraguan Revolution is all about: empowering men and women with the educational and economic weapons that will permit them to become agents of their own history, and to construct their future in a way that reflects their collective needs as a nation. This is what the Grenadians sought to accomplish, and this is indeed the goal toward which the people of South Africa are striving.

As we continue to fight for the right to build and expand ethnic studies programs, we have much to learn from the people who are struggling for and defending the achievements of their national liberation. There are also lessons to be learned from the experiences of the socialist countries in general. The entire world is involved in a process of transformation, which is gradually rendering defunct the socioeconomic structures of capitalism. Whether consciously or not, the struggles of racially and nationally oppressed people in the United States are tied to the efforts of people across the globe to hasten that process. And whether we acknowledge it or not, our own defense of ethnic studies contains this world-historical dynamic. As Dr. Martin Luther King, Jr., declared just before his assassination in 1968:

> These are revolutionary times; all over the globe men [and women!] are revolting against old systems of exploitation and oppression. The shirtless and barefoot people of the land are rising up as never before. "The people that walked in darkness have seen a great light." We in the West must support these revolutions. . . . We must find new ways to speak for peace in Vietnam and for justice throughout the developing world, a world that borders on our doors. If we do not act, we shall surely be dragged down the long, dark and shameful corridors of time reserved for those who possess power without compassion, might without morality, and strength without sight.[10]

NOTES

1. W.E.B. DuBois, *Dusk of Dawn* (New York: Schocken Books, 1968), pp. 116–17.

2. "Spotlight on Soweto," in *Peace Courier*. Information Center of the World Peace Council. Helsinki, Finland: February 1984.

3. Ibid.

4. Ibid.

5. Maurice Bishop, *Maurice Bishop Speaks* (New York: Pathfinder Press, 1983), p. 42.

6. *Grenada Is Not Alone*, speeches by the People's Revolutionary Government at the 1st International Conference in Solidarity With Grenada,

November 1981 (St. Georges, Grenada: Fedon Publishers, 1982), p. 51.

7. Ibid., p. 60.

8. Peter Rosset and John Vandemeer, eds., *The Nicaragua Reader* (New York: Grove Press, 1983), p. 347.

9. Fernando Cardenal and Valerie Miller, "Nicaragua 1980: The Battle of the ABCs" in Armand Mattelart, ed., *Communicating in Nicaragua* (New York: International General, 1986), pp. 97–98.

10. Martin Luther King, Jr., *Trumpet of Conscience* (New York: Harper and Row, 1968), pp. 33–34.

Art on the Frontline: Mandate for a People's Culture

In 1951, Paul Robeson made the following declaration at a Conference in New York City organized around the theme of equal rights for Negroes in the arts, sciences and professions:

> There are despoilers abroad in our land, akin to those who attempted to throttle our Republic at its birth. Despoilers who would have kept my beloved people in unending serfdom, a powerful few who blessed Hitler as he destroyed a large segment of a great people . . .
>
> All [the] millions of the world stand aghast at the sight and the name of *America*—but they love *us*; they look to *us* to help create a world where we can all live in peace and friendship, where we can exchange the excellence of our various arts and crafts, the manifold wonders of our mutual scientific creations, a world where we can rejoice at the unleashed power of our innermost selves, of the potential of

—Originally published under the title "For a People's Culture," in *Political Affairs* LXVIV, no. 3, March 1985.

great masses of people. To them *we* are the real America. Let us remember that.

And let us learn how to bring to the great masses of the American people *our* culture and *our* art. For in the end, what are we talking about when we talk about American culture today? We are talking about a culture that is restricted to the very, very few. How many workers ever get to the theatre? I was in concerts for 20 years, subscription concerts, the two thousand seats gone before any Negro in the community, any worker, could even hear about a seat. . . . Only by going into the trade unions and singing on the picket lines and in the struggles for the freedom of our people—only in this way could the workers of this land hear me.[1]

More than three decades later, this problem articulated by Paul Robeson still remains one of the main challenges facing progressive artists and political activists: How do we collectively acknowledge our popular cultural legacy and communicate it to the masses of our people, most of whom have been denied access to the social spaces reserved for art and culture? In the United States, a rich and vibrant tradition of people's art has emerged from the history of labor militancy and the struggles of Afro-Americans, women, and peace activists. It is essential that we explore that tradition, understand it, reclaim it, and glean from it the cultural nourishment that can assist us in preparing a political and cultural counteroffensive against the regressive institutions and ideas spawned by advanced monopoly capitalism.

As Marx and Engels long ago observed, art is a form of social consciousness—a special form of social consciousness that can potentially awaken an urge in those affected by it to creatively transform their oppressive environments. Art can function as a sensitizer and a catalyst, propelling people toward involvement in organized movements seeking to effect radical social change. Art is special because of its ability to influence feelings as well as knowledge. Christopher Cauldwell, the British Communist who wrote extensively on aesthetics, once defined the function of art as the socializing of the human instincts and the educating of human emotions:

> Emotion, in all its vivid coloring, is the creation of ages of culture acting on the blind, unfeeling instincts. All art, all education, all day-to-day social experience, draw it out . . . and direct and shape its myriad phenomena.[2]

Progressive art can assist people to learn not only about the objective forces at work in the society in which they live, but also about the intensely social character of their interior lives. Ultimately, it can propel people toward social emancipation. While not all progressive art need be concerned with explicitly political problems—indeed, a love song can be progressive if it incorporates a sensitivity toward the lives of working-class women and men—I want to specifically explore overt sociopolitical meanings in art with the purpose of defining the role art can play in hastening social progress.

Because the history of Afro-American culture reveals strong bonds between art and the struggle for Black liberation, it holds important lessons for those who are interested in strengthening the bridges between art and people's movements today. Of all the art forms historically associated with Afro-American culture, music has played the greatest catalytic role in awakening social consciousness in the community. During the era of slavery, Black people were victims of a conscious strategy of cultural genocide, which proscribed the practice of virtually all African customs with the exception of music. If slaves were permitted to sing as they toiled in the fields and to incorporate music into their religious services, it was because the slaveocracy failed to grasp the social function of music in general and particularly the central role music played in all aspects of life in West African society. As a result, Black people were able to create with their music an aesthetic community of resistance, which in turn encouraged and nurtured a political community of active struggle for freedom. This continuum of struggle, which is at once aesthetic and political, has extended from Harriet Tubman's and Nat Turner's spirituals through Bessie Smith's "Poor Man's Blues" and Billie Holiday's "Strange Fruit," through Max Roach's "Freedom Suite," and even to the progressive raps on the popular music scene of the 1980's.

With the Afro-American spiritual, a language of struggle was forged that was as easily understood by the slaves as it was misinterpreted by the slaveholders. While the slaveocracy attempted to establish absolute authority over the slaves' individual and communal lives, the spirituals were both cause and evidence of an autonomous political consciousness. These songs formed a complex language that both incorporated and called forth a deep yearning for freedom. When the slaves sang, "Didn't My Lord Deliver Daniel and Why Not Every Man?," they utilized religious themes to symbolize their own concrete predicament and their own worldly desire to be free. When they sang "Samp-

son Tore the Building Down," they made symbolic refer-
ence to their desire to see the oppressive edifice of slavery
come crashing down.

> If I had my way,
> O Lordy, Lordy,
> If I had my way;
> If I had my way,
> I would tear this building down.

Oftentimes the religious music of the slaves played real
and instrumental roles in the operation of the underground
railroad and in the organization of antislavery insurrections.
The lyrics of "Follow the Drinking Gourd," for example,
literally provided a map of one section of the underground
railroad, and "Steal Away to Jesus" was a coded song ral-
lying together those engaged in the organization of Nat
Turner's rebellion. But even when the spirituals were not
linked to specific actions in the freedom struggle, they always served, epistemologically and psychologically, to
shape the consciousness of the masses of Black people, guar-
anteeing that the fires of freedom would burn within them.
As Sidney Finkelstein pointed out,

> The antislavery struggle was the core of the struggle for
> democracy, so spirituals embodied in their music and poetry
> the affirmation of an unbreakable demand for freedom.[3]

The spirituals have directly influenced the music associated with other people's movements at various moments in
the history of the United States. Many songs of the labor
and peace movements have their origins in the religious

music of the slaves, and the "freedom songs" of the Civil Rights Movement were spirituals whose lyrics were sometimes slightly altered in order to reflect more concretely the realities of that struggle.

Even the blues, frequently misrepresented as a music form focusing on trivial aspects of sexual love, are closely tied to Black people's strivings for freedom. In the words of James Cone:

> For many people, a blues song is about sex or a lonely woman longing for her rambling man. However, the blues are more than that. To be sure, the blues involve sex and what that means for human bodily expression, but on a much deeper level . . . the blues express a black perspective on the incongruity of life and the attempt to achieve meaning in a situation fraught with contradictions. As Aunt Molly Jackson of Kentucky put it: "The blues are made by working people . . . when they have a lot of problems to solve about their work, when their wages are low . . . and they don't know which way to turn and what to do."[4]

And, indeed, Bessie Smith, the Empress of the Blues, reached the apex of her career when she composed and recorded a song transmitting an unmistakable political message, entitled "Poor Man's Blues." This song evoked the exploitation and manipulation of working people by the wealthy and portrayed the rich as parasites accumulating their wealth and fighting their wars with the labor of the poor.

Another pinnacle in the evolution of Afro-American music was Billie Holiday's incorporation of the political anti-lynching song "Strange Fruit" into her regular repertoire.

Throughout Lady Day's career, thousands of people were compelled to confront the brutal realities of southern racism, even as they sought to escape the problems of everyday life through music, alcohol, and the ambiance of smoke-filled nightclubs. Undoubtedly, some went on to actively participate in the antilynching movement of that era.

That Billie Holiday recorded "Strange Fruit" in 1939 was no accident. Neither was the fact that the lyrics of this song were composed by progressive poet Lewis Allan, who was associated with activist struggles of the 1930's. The thirties remain the most exciting and exuberant period in the evolution of American cultural history. The process of developing a mature people's art movement today can be facilitated by a serious examination of that era's achievements. As Phillip Bonosky points out in a 1959 *Political Affairs* article entitled "The Thirties in American Culture":

> There is every reason in the world why official reaction should want the thirties to be forgotten as if they never existed. For that period remains a watershed in the American democratic tradition. It is a period which will continue to serve both the present and the future as a reminder and as an example of how an aroused people, led and spurred on by the working class, can change the entire complexion of the culture of a nation.[5]

Bourgeois ideologists have consequently attempted to

> . . . misrepresent and burn out of the consciousness of the American people, and first of all the artists and intellectuals, the fact that the making of a people's culture once did exist in the United States and was inspired, to a large degree, by

the working class, often led, and largely influenced, by the Communist Party.[6]

Answering the charges leveled against the Communist party that it "belittles and vulgarizes the rule of culture," Bonosky argues that no other political party in the entire history of this country had ever manifested such a serious concern for art. The Communist party was involved, for example, in the 1935 Call for an American Writers' Congress—which claimed Langston Hughes, Theodore Dreiser, Richard Wright, and Erskine Caldwell among its signers. As a result of the work of the Communist party and other progressive forces, artists won the right to work as artists in projects under the auspices of the Works Progress Administration. What the WPA artists accomplished was an unprecedented achievement in the history of the United States: Art was brought to the people on a truly massive scale. It could no longer be confined to the private domain, monopolized by those whose class background made galleries, museums, theaters and concert halls routinely accessible. For the first time, American art became public art. This meant, for example, that working-class people utilizing the services of the post office could simultaneously appreciate the public murals painted there. Sculpture, music, and theater were among the other arts directly taken to the people during that era. Moreover, to quote Bonosky once more, when these programs were threatened with dissolution,

> . . . it was the Communist Party that struggled so heroically to save the art projects and with them of course the theory that art was responsible to the people of which these projects were the living embodiment. For the first time in American

history artists and writers walked picket lines in the name of
and in the defense of the right of artists to *be* artists. [7]

The radical approach to art and culture inspired by the
Communist party and other Left forces during the Great
Depression involved more than the forging of an art that
was publicly accessible to the masses. Much of the art of
that period was people's art in the sense that artists learned
how to pay attention to the material and emotional lives of
working people in America in the process of working out
the content of their aesthetic creations. Meridel LeSeuer explored the lives of working people in her literature as Woody
Guthrie composed songs about their lives and struggles.
This emerging people's art was therefore a challenge to the
dominant bourgeois culture. Artists not only felt compelled
to defend their right to communicate the real pains, joys,
and aspirations of the working class through their art, but
many went on to become activists in the labor struggles and
in the fight for the rights of the unemployed and especially
of Black people. In the process, of course, new artists were
summoned up from the ranks of these struggles.

Bourgeois aesthetics has always sought to situate art in a
transcendant realm, beyond ideology, beyond socioeconomic realities, and certainly beyond the class struggle. In
an infinite variety of ways, art has been represented as the
pure subjective product of individual creativity. Lenin's 1905
article "Party Organization and Party Literature" challenged
this vision of art and developed the principle of partisanship
in art and literature—a principle with which many progressive artists of the 1930's were, at least implicitly, in
agreement. Lenin made it absolutely clear that in insisting

that aesthetic creations be partisan, he was not advocating the dictatorship of the party over art and literature.

> There is no question that literature is least of all subject to mechanical adjustment or leveling to the rule of the majority over the minority. There is no question either that in this field greater scope must undoubtedly be allowed for personal initiative, individual inclination, thought and fantasy, form and content.[8]

He pointed out, however, that the bourgeois demand for abstract subjective freedom in art was actually a stifling of the freedom of creativity. Literature and art, he said, must be free not only from police censorship,

> . . . but from capital, from careerism, and . . . bourgeois anarchist individualism. Partisan literature and art will be truly free, because it will further the freedom of millions of people.[9]

What are the current prospects for the further expansion of an art that is not afraid to declare its partisan relationship to people's struggles for economic, racial, and sexual equality? Not only must we acknowledge and defend the cultural legacy that has been transmitted to us over the decades, but we must also be in a position to recognize the overt as well as subtle hints of progressive developments in popular art forms today. Over the last several years, for example, such partisan films as *Silkwood* and *Missing* have emerged as beacons amid the routinely mediocre, sexist, violent, and generally antihuman values characterizing most products of the Hollywood cinema industry.

To consider another art form, some of the superstars of popular-musical culture today are unquestionably musical geniuses, but they have distorted the Black music tradition by brilliantly developing its form while ignoring its content of struggle and freedom. Nonetheless, there is illumination to be found in contemporary Black music in the works of such artists as Stevie Wonder and Gil Scott-Heron, who have acknowledged the legacy of Black music in form and content alike. Their individual creations have awakened in their audiences a true sense of the dignity of human freedom.

Stevie Wonder's tune "Happy Birthday" touched the hearts of hundreds of thousands of young people, mobilizing them in support of the movement to declare Dr. Martin Luther King, Jr.'s birthday a national holiday. That Reagan was forced to sign the bill enacting that law, despite his openly articulated opposition, demonstrated that popular sentiment could prevail over the most intransigent official racism this country has known in many years.

Gil Scott-Heron's immensely popular song "B-Movie," released shortly after Reagan was elected to his first term, mobilized strong anti-Reagan sentiments in young Black public opinion. The song-poem particularly exposed the efforts of the Reagan propagandists to declare that he had received a "mandate" from the people.

> The first thing I want to say is "mandate"
>   my ass
> Because it seems as though we've been convinced
> That 26% of the registered voters
> Not even 26% of the American people

Form a mandate or a landslide . . .
But, oh yeah, I remember . . .
I remember what I said about Reagan
Acted like an actor/Hollyweird
Acted like a liberal
Acted like General Franco
When he acted like governor of California
Then he acted like a Republican
Then he acted like somebody was going
   to vote for him for president
And now he acts like 26% of the registered voters
Is actually a mandate
We're all actors in this, actually

Bruce Springsteen's album *Born in the USA* was lauded
by Reagan, who praised "the message of hope in the songs
. . . of New Jersey's own Bruce Springsteen" as he cam-
paigned in that state for the presidency in 1984. However,
Reagan's aides more than likely simply assumed that
Springsteen's red, white, and blue album cover indicated
acceptance of the fraudulent patriotism promoted by the
Reagan administration. Two days after Reagan's remark,
Springsteen introduced a song entitled "Johnny 99" by saying, "I don't think the president was listening to this one,"
going on to sing about a desperate, debt-ridden, unemployed autoworker who landed on death row after killing
someone in the course of a robbery. Another one of his
songs, "My Hometown," is about the devastation wrought
by plant shutdowns:

Now Mainstreet's whitewashed windows
   and vacant stores
Seems like there ain't nobody wants to come

down here no more
They're closing down the textile mill across
   the railroad tracks
Foreman says these jobs are going, boys,
   and they ain't coming back
To your hometown . . .

A new genre of music with roots in the age-old tradition of storytelling has gained increasing popularity among the youth of today. Rap music clearly reflects the daily lives of working-class people, particularly urban Afro-American and Latino youth. Many rap songs incorporate a progressive consciousness of current political affairs as revealed, for example, by the following rap by Grand Master Flash and Melle Mel which calls upon youth to associate themselves with the Reverend Jesse Jackson's 1984 campaign for the presidency:

Oh beautiful for spacious skies
And your amber waves of untold lies
Look at all the politicians trying to do a job
But they can't help but look like the mob
Get a big kickback, put it away
Watch the FBI watch the CIA
They want a bigger missile and a faster jet
But yet they forgot to hire the vets

Hypocrites and Uncle Toms are talking trash
   Let's talk about Jesse
Liberty and Justice are a thing of the past
   Let's talk about Jesse
They want a stronger nation at any cost
   Let's talk about Jesse

> Even if it means that everything will soon be lost
>> Let's talk about Jesse
> He started on the bottom, now he's on the top
>> Let's talk about Jesse
> He proved that he can make it, so don't ever stop
>
> Now let's stand together and let the whole world see
> Our brother Jesse Jackson go down in history
> So vote, vote, vote
> Everybody get up and vote. . . .

Young people are becoming more and more conscious of the need to oppose the nuclear-arms race. A rap tune popularized by Harry Belafonte's film *Beat Street* contains the following warning:

> A newspaper burns in the sand
> And the headlines say man the story's bad
> Extra extra read all the bad news
> On the war or peace
> That everybody would lose
> The rise and fall of the last great empire
> The sound of the whole world caught on fire
> The ruthless struggle the desperate gamble
> The games that left the whole world in shambles
> The cheats the lies the alibis
> And the foolish attempt to conquer the skies
> Lost in space and what is it worth
> The president just forgot about earth
> Spending all time billions and maybe even trillions
> Because the weapons ran in the zillions . . .
> A fight for power a nuclear shower
> The people shout out in the darkest hour
> It's sights unseen and voices unheard

And finally the bomb gets the last word . . .
. . . We've got to suffer when things get rougher
And that's the reason why we've got to get tougher
So learn from the past and work for the future
Don't be a slave to no computer
'Cause the children of man inherit the land
And the future of the world is in your hands

While numerous examples of progressive trends in contemporary popular music might be proposed, it would be a gross misconstruction of the music industry to argue that such songs are representative of what young people are hearing on the airwaves today. In general, the popular-musical culture that greets young people has been rigorously molded by the demands of the capitalist marketplace, which measures its products according to their profit-making potential. While progressive messages sometimes manage to slip through the net of capitalist production, by and large the musical culture it advances promotes reified sexuality, crass individualism, and often violent, sexist, antiworking-class values. Many talented musicians ultimately destroy their artistic potential as they attempt to create music that conforms to what is deemed salable by the market. As Marx pointed out long ago in *Theories of Surplus Value*, "capitalist production is hostile to certain branches of spiritual production, namely poetry and art."[10]

We cannot expect mass popular art to express stronger and more efficacious progressive themes without the further development of an art movement philosophically and organizationally allied with people's struggles. In recent years, conscious political art has become increasingly evident. The importance of the Chicago Peace Museum, for example, should not be underestimated. Nor should the development of the national movement Artists' Call Against Intervention in Central America. This mobilization, which spread to twenty-five cities across the country, came as a response to an appeal from the Sandinista Cultural Workers' Association:

> May it go down in the history of humanity that one day during the twentieth century, in the face of the gigantic aggression that one of the smallest countries of the world, Nicaragua, was about to suffer, artists and intellectuals of different nationalities and generations raised along with us the banner of fraternity, in order to prevent our total destruction.[11]

In San Francisco alone, over two hundred artists participated in three major exhibitions. Funds collected nationwide by this movement were donated to the Association of Cultural Workers in Nicaragua, the University of El Salvador, a labor union in El Salvador, and to Guatemalan refugees. Another artists' movement in solidarity with Central America that emerged in the San Francisco Bay Area chose the name of PLACA, which means to make a mark, to leave a sign. They dedicated an entire street of murals with the theme of opposition to U.S. intervention in Central America. In their manifesto, the artists and muralists proclaim:

> PLACA members do not ally themselves with this Administration's policy that has created death and war and despair, and that threatens more lives daily. We aim to demonstrate in visual/environmental terms, our solidarity, our respect, for the people of Central America.[12]

Similar to Artists' Call, a cultural movement in opposition to U.S. support for the racist and fascist policies of the South African government declared October 1984 Art Against Apartheid month. Exhibitions and cultural events advocating involvement in the campaign to free Nelson Mandela and all political prisoners in South Africa and Namibia were held throughout the New York City area and in other cities across the country. At the San Francisco Art Institute, a group of artists associated with the Art Against Apartheid movement organized a month-long festival in the spring of 1985 in solidarity with the people of South Africa.

One of the most exciting progressive cultural developments is the song movement, which has built musical bridges between the labor movement, the Afro-American movement, the solidarity struggles with Central America and South Africa, and the peace movement. Such politically committed musicians as Sweet Honey in the Rock, Holly Near, and Casselberry-Dupreé, have brought a keen awareness of these struggles into the women's movement. Bernice Johnson Reagon of Sweet Honey in the Rock has published numerous articles and delivered speeches appealing to those who support women's music to associate themselves with working-class struggles, antiracist movements, peace struggles, and solidarity work. And anyone familiar with Sweet Honey's songs can attest to the fact that they effectively and poignantly promote these coalition politics. Occupational health hazards—asbestosis, silicosis, brown-lung and black-lung disease—are the themes of "More Than a Paycheck," for example. In other songs, Sweet Honey evokes the civil-rights leader Fannie Lou Hamer and the murdered South African activist Steven Biko, and Mexican immigrants who fall prey to the repressive immigration laws of the United

States. A recurring theme in their music is the need for all people to join together to prevent the outbreak of a nuclear war.

Sisterfire, the annual women's music festival in which Sweet Honey in the Rock has played an instrumental role, attempts to actualize the concept of coalition politics through cultural vehicles. In one of its manifestos, Sisterfire was described as

> a salutation to all women, working people, minorities and the poor who stand fast against dehumanizing political and economic systems. [13]

Moreover,

> culture, in its most valid form, expresses a mass or popular character. It must not be defined and perpetuated by an elite few for the benefit of a few. Culture must, of necessity, reflect and chart humanity's attempt to live in harmony with itself and nature. . . . We are building bridges between the women's movement and other movements for progressive social change. We are playing with fire, and we want nothing less from this event than to set loose the creative, fierce and awesome energies in all of you. [14]

Holly Near, who has been associated for many years with the women's music movement as well as with many other people's struggles, continues to encourage musicians to move beyond narrow social and political concerns and to promote justice for women and men of all races and nationalities. In 1984, she and Ronnie Gilbert did a "Dump Reagan" tour, which took them to twenty-five cities where they sang to over twenty-five thousand people. Another exemplary action in the bridge-building effort undertaken by the women's music movement was the song written by Betsy Rose for the mayoral campaign of Black activist Mel King in Boston, entitled "We May Have Come Here on Different Ships, but We're in the Same Boat Now."

Within the development of this song movement, Communists have played important roles. The Ad Hoc Singers, for example, who first came together during the 1980 presidential campaign, have brought to the movement songs that deepen the class consciousness of those who experience them. Their "People Before Profits," introduced during the first anti-Reagan campaign, is a virtual anthem of people's struggles. What is perhaps most important about the Ad Hoc Singers is that they bring to the song movement a dimension of concrete, activist experience in these struggles.

And, indeed, if we can anticipate the further expansion of people's culture today, it will be a direct function of the deepening and growing influence of mass movements. Progressive and revolutionary art is inconceivable outside of the context of political movements for radical change. If bold new art forms emerged with the Russian Revolution, the Cuban Revolution, and more recently the Sandinista and Grenada Revolutions, then we can be certain that if we accomplish the task before us today of strengthening and uniting our mass movements, our cultural life will flourish. Cultural workers must thus be concerned not only with the creation of progressive art, but must be actively involved in the organization of people's political movements. An exemplary relationship between art and struggle has been at the very core of the journal *Freedomways*—not only does it serve as a vehicle for the dissemination of progressive Black literature, but it actively participates in the political struggles of Afro-Americans and their allies.

If cultural workers utilize their talents on an ever-increasing scale to accomplish the task of awakening and sensitizing people to the need for a mass challenge to the ultraright, the prospects for strengthening and further uniting the antimonopoly movement, bringing together labor, Afro-Americans, women, and peace activists will greatly increase. As that movement wins victories, existing artists will draw inspiration from the creative energy of this process, and new artists will emerge as a result. If we are able to set this dynamic in motion, we will begin to move securely in the direction of economic, racial, and sexual emancipation—indeed, toward the ultimate goal of socialism—and we will be able to anticipate a peaceful future, free of the threat of nuclear war.

NOTES

1. Paul Robeson, *Paul Robeson Speaks* (New Jersey: Citadel Press, 1978), p. 303–304.

2. Christopher Caudwell, *Studies in a Dying Culture* (New York: Monthly Review Press, 1971), p. 183.

3. Sidney Finkelstein, *How Music Expresses Ideas* (New York: International Press, 1971), p. 118.

4. James Cone, *The Spirituals and the Blues* (New York: Seabury Press, 1972), pp. 115–16.

5. Phillip Bonosky, "The Thirties," *Political Affairs*, January 1959.

6. Ibid.

7. Ibid.

8. V. I. Lenin, "Party Organization and Party Literature," in *Lenin on Literature and Art* (Moscow: Progress Publishers, 1970), p. 24.

9. Ibid.

10. *Marx and Engels on Literature and Art* (Moscow: Progress Publishers, 1976), p. 141.

11. "Artists Call Against Intervention in Central America" (brochure, San Francisco, 1984).

12. PLACA Mural Group: General Statement (in brochure issued by PLACA San Francisco, 1985).

13. "Sisterfire: Statement of Purpose" (leaflet issued by Sisterfire. Washington, D.C.: 1982).

14. Ibid.

Underexposed:
Photography and
Afro-American History

In 1969, the Metropolitan Museum of Art presented an exhibition entitled "Harlem on My Mind: Cultural Capital of Black America, 1900–1968." According to its coordinator, Allon Schoener, the exhibition

> . . . could be one of the most important . . . to have been presented in an art museum in the twentieth century because it redefined the role and responsibility of museums, their audiences, and the types of exhibitions they could present.[1]

Nonetheless, Black community activists organized a protest to mark the opening of the show. Among those who marched on the picket line was Roy DeCarava, one of the most prominent Afro-American photographers of the time,

—Originally published under the title "Photography and Afro-American History," in Valencia Hollins Coar, *A Century of Black American Photographers, 1840–1960* (Providence: Rhode Island School of Design, 1983), to accompany an exhibition of the same title at the school's Museum of Art, March 31–May 8, 1983.

who strongly challenged the merits of "Harlem on My Mind."

> It is evident from the physical makeup of the show that Schoener and company have no respect for or understanding of photography, or, for that matter, any of the other media that they employed. I would also say that they have no great love for or understanding of Harlem, Black people or history.[2]

The controversy unleashed by this exhibition—which was no doubt a sincere attempt to break the cycle of racism within the U.S. art establishment—revealed deeper influences of racism even on apparently progressive cultural perceptions and definitions.

If it were possible to consider "Harlem on My Mind"—the exhibition and the subsequently published book—an unqualified success, even this would not have begun to reverse the conspicuous sparsity of images depicting Afro-American life within the recorded history of photography. There have indeed been a few important moments such as Frances Benjamin Johnston's photographic documentation of Hampton Institute around the turn of the century or W. Eugene Smith's 1951 photo-essay in *Life* entitled "Nurse-Midwife." Yet such glimpses of Black life have incorporated the vision of white artists, necessarily outsiders to the culture that their images attempt to capture. From the era of photography's emergence up to the present period, Black photographers have been forcibly and systematically rendered invisible. "One of the few positive effects of 'Harlem on My Mind,'" according to photography critic A. D. Coleman, "was that it brought to the attention of critics and public alike the work of James Van Der Zee."[3] Van Der Zee, Gordon Parks, and Roy DeCarava (the latter having refused to participate in the Harlem show) are among the very few whose names have recently begun to be recognizable. Not one of them, however—not a single Afro-American photographer, in fact—has been included in the most current authoritative history of the medium to be published in the United States.[4] Thus, the momentous character of the present assemblage of eleven decades of Black photography.

Many will find it astonishing that Black people became involved in photography shortly after the invention of the daguerreotype: Jules Lion, who became acquainted with this process in France, may well have introduced it to the city of New Orleans. But, then, how many prominent scientists, scholars, and artists have been banished from historical records for no other reason than their racial heritage, only to be revealed, shamefully late, as outstanding contributors in their fields? Jules Lion, Robert Duncanson and J. P. Ball ought not now to evoke new responses of surprise. Rather, they should be celebrated as evidence of what knowledgeable persons should have strongly suspected all along. Yes, Black photographers were active during the very earliest stages of their medium's history. Granted, there were but a few, for slavery imposed a historical prohibition on virtually all forms of open aesthetic creation; only music, misunderstood as it was by the slaveocracy, was permitted to flourish. But what about the untapped artistic potential of those millions of slaves? Do we dare imagine how many pioneering Black photographers there might have been had more favorable socioeconomic circumstances prevailed?

Perhaps a less speculative question should be considered: What was the posture of early Black photographers toward the collective predicament of Afro-American people? "The innate love of harmony and beauty," wrote W.E.B. DuBois,

> that set the ruder souls of his people a-dancing and a-singing raised but confusion and doubt in the soul of the black artist; for the beauty revealed to him was the soul-beauty of a race which his larger audience despised, and he could not articulate the message of another people.[5]

Could this be the reason why the works and careers of the few early photographers appear entirely removed from the situations and aspirations of the masses of Afro-Americans? Where, in the works of daguerreotypist Jules Lion, was the Black population's powerful yearning for freedom to be found? Did the photographic images of his Black contemporaries and immediate successors bear witness, in any discernible manner, to the common dreams of an enslaved people, whose songs and struggles focused on their collective liberation? If these questions cannot be answered unreservedly in the affirmative, it is due, no doubt, to the pressures exerted by that "larger audience" to which DuBois refers. Black people, the vast majority of whom were slaves prior to 1863, were simply not considered appropriate subjects of serious visual art. Indeed, this was no less true for Afro-American painters, sculptors, and photographers than for their white contemporaries.

The paucity of distinctive Black features in the works of early Black photographers should not be misconstrued as permission to dismiss the issue of these artists' relationship to the collective experience of their race. However they subjectively chose to address—or ignore—the racial politics of their times, they could hardly avoid being influenced in some way by objective historical conditions. And there were turbulent stirrings in the Black population and among their white allies during the decade that closed with the invention of the daguerreotype. There was Nat Turner's awesome slave rebellion of 1831 and the founding conference, two years later, of the American Anti-Slavery Society. By 1837, there were also white martyrs, like the abolitionist newspaperman Elijah P. Lovejoy, viciously murdered by a racist mob in Illinois. The next year, a momentous escape occurred, effected by the slave soon to be known as Frederick Douglass, the eloquent orator and powerful abolitionist leader. This was also the year when the Black antislavery activist Robert Purvis formally organized the Underground Railroad.

If this was an era when the Black pursuit of freedom emerged as one of the nation's dominant social concerns, it was also a period of vibrant and prolific artistic expressions related to the antislavery cause. At the same time as George Mose Horton published his "Poems of a Slave," Longfellow's "Poems on Slavery" also appeared. Although this was apparently an exceptional case, there was an Afro-American visual artist, the engraver and lithographer Patrick Reason, who devoted much of his work to abolitionist themes. "Reason spoke out vehemently against slavery, devoting much of his time to illustrating abolitionist literature."[6] His portrait of Henry Bibb, author of one of the epoch's popular slave narratives, expressed a certain determination to link the work of Black visual artists—like their people's literature and still unrecognized musical creations—to the race's historic social striving for liberation.

It is a great misfortune that the racist requirements of

"American" art excluded Black slaves in a virtually a priori fashion as potential subjects of serious visual art, for an abundance of profoundly inspiring material could have been gleaned from their lives and deeds, material waiting to be shaped by the artist's hand into exciting new creations. Consider, for example, the fascinating case of Henry "Box" Brown, the slave who escaped inside a box that was shipped to the North by operators of the Underground Railroad. And the dramatic escape by William and Ellen Craft in 1849: Ellen, passing for white, donned male attire and posed as her husband's master. The couple successfully traveled from Georgia to the free city of Philadelphia. While Harriet Tubman's escape that same year was not itself distinctively dramatic, its consequences were earthshaking and historic. Countless freedom treks were led by this fearless woman, destined to become her people's Moses.

The Afro-American photographer J. P. Ball was active during the 1850's. One is tempted to speculate about the extent to which he and others were touched by the feats of freedom fighters like Harriet Tubman. While concrete answers must await further specific historical research, it is clear that by the 1850's, the issue of slavery had emphatically moved to the center of national attention. It had become a question that no one, Black or white—and especially not scholars and cultural workers—could be permitted to ignore. Indeed, one of the era's most popular pieces of literature was *Uncle Tom's Cabin*, the crusading antislavery novel by Harriet Beecher Stowe. The very popularity of Stowe's work was irrefutable evidence of the novel's outstanding role in defending the abolitionist cause. Yet it was also responsible for popularizing social attitudes toward Black people that seemingly contradicted its progressive, antislavery intent. For even as it encouraged Black people's right to be free, it legitimized and gave definitive, popular form to stereotypical notions of racial inferiority. In fact, precisely the process through which Stowe's novel evoked a popular revulsion toward slavery also furnished the literary weapons for an ideological victory—however unintentional—of racism.

Uncle Tom's Cabin facilitated—not alone, but in a major sense—the increasingly deeper penetration of racist images and attitudes into the country's cultural life. Consider an 1883 painting entitled "Uncle Tom and Little Eva" and its depiction of a large but obviously helpless Black man who looks to an angelic little white girl for light and direction. This painting, which incorporates Stowe's stereotypes in their original forms, is not the work of a naive white artist, as might be suspected. Rather, it was produced by Afro-American Robert Scott Duncanson. And Duncanson was not the only one to be inspired in this fashion to project unintentionally destructive images of his people. Yet Afro-Americans had also furnished the means with which to expose the racist distortions in Stowe's portrayal of Black people, for by that time the slave narrative had become a well-established literary genre. Solomon Northrup and Frederick Douglass, for example, had presented firsthand accounts of their lives, their sufferings, and their hopes under the "peculiar institution." Black people's burgeoning literary creations at midcentury included the works of William Wells Brown, who went on, after authoring a slave narrative, to become Afro-America's first novelist and playwright. Among poets at midcentury, Frances E. W. Harper was destined to receive the widest acclaim for her work. While she herself was born "free," she wrote her most brilliant and celebrated verse on the righteous struggles of her enslaved people—poems, for example, like "The Slave Auction" and "Bury Me in a Free Land." Such was the flourishing and often militant literary context within which midcentury Black photographers—whether consciously or not—pursued their potentially powerful craft. Like their colleagues who wielded the pen, they possessed the ability to utilize the camera to forge creative, affirmative images of their people.

> There came the slow looming of emancipation. Crowds and armies of the unknown, inscrutable, unfathomable Yankees; cruelly behind and before; rumors of a new slave trade; but slowly, continuously, the wild truth, a bitter truth, the magic truth, came surging through.
>
> There was to be a new freedom! . . . They prayed; they worked; they danced and sang; they studied to learn; they wanted to wander.[7]

Slavery was banned from history, but while Black people certainly felt the falling of their chains, they also soon realized that they had by no means achieved their collective goal of liberation. If a new promise was later offered, during the years of Radical Reconstruction, it would be abruptly snatched away by the Hayes-Tilden Compromise of 1877, which ushered in a period of pervasive, destructive racism. Segregation was legalized in the South, and the population of former slaves began to suffer systematic disenfranchisement. Mob violence and lynchings claimed countless lives, while the use of racist terror and other tactics of intimidation became the routine approach to Black peasants and workers adopted by white officials and employers in the South. In

1890, for example, there were 85 reported lynchings, 112 in 1891 and 160 in 1892—and, as the last years of the century rolled by, this wave of racist violence would continue to swell.

This was the sociohistorical background against which the lives and careers of such photographic artists as Harry Shephard and Hamilton S. Smith evolved. As they worked with their cameras, selecting their subjects, composing their images, how were they affected by the raging violence of racist mobs, those massacres of Black people euphemistically known as "race riots"? Were the images they recorded influenced at all by the knowledge that untold thousands of Black bodies had hung from trees or gone up in flames at the stake? Their literary contemporary Charles Chesnutt published a novel in 1901 entitled *The Marrow of Tradition*, based directly on the 1898 massacre in Wilmington, North Carolina. Were any Afro-American photographers inspired by Chesnutt's example?

By the beginning of the twentieth century, photography in the United States and Europe had entered its historical state of maturity. Mathew Brady had photographed the Civil War, Timothy H. O'Sullivan had conducted expeditions to photograph remote areas of the West. And countless millions of human portraits had been recorded on film. According to the census of 1900, at least 247 Afro-Americans were professional photographers. Of course, it can be assumed that the vast majority concentrated their work on studio portraits, but if James Van Der Zee is at all typical, many, like him, photographed street scenes, parades, political rallies, and whatever might have been transpiring in their immediate world. A. D. Coleman reports that during most of his career, Van Der Zee

. . . was entirely unaware of what was happening in the medium, even of what was going on with Black photographers; such names as Steichen, Stieglitz, Hine and van Vechten rang no bells in his memory.[8]

Yet was it really necessary to be familiar, for example, with Jacob Riis's images of the poor and their environment in order to move toward the photographic documentation of oppression? Was it necessary for Black photographers to look toward white models in order to recognize that photography could be a profoundly social art form, capable of generating human urges toward progressive change?

To continue the line of questioning begun above, did any of the early twentieth-century Black photographers attempt to record images reflecting the omnipresent and devastating racism of those years? How did Black photography address the 1906 race riots in Springfield, Ohio, and Atlanta, Georgia—and the notorious assaults the same year on Black soldiers in Brownsville, Texas? Were any visual challenges inspired by the 1916 lynching of Jesse Washington, who was burned to death in Waco, Texas, before a cheering crowd of fifteen thousand white people—men, women, and even children? Included in the "Harlem on My Mind" exhibition was a photograph of a march in Harlem protesting the East Saint Louis race riots of 1917. How many more images remain to be discovered that evoke the presence of and resistance to the terrible violence of 1917 and the murderous Red Summer of 1919?

With the rise of the film industry during the first decades of the twentieth century, racist stereotypes began to acquire definitive perceptual forms, a process that was masterfully executed in D. W. Griffith's *Birth of a Nation*. What Afro-

American photographers sought to forge true Black images, pictures whose creative power could expose and condemn the evolving visual mythology of racism? Certainly James Van Der Zee's impressive Black imagery provides affirmative, realistic evidence of the urbanized Afro-American, and specifically the inhabitants of Harlem during the 1920's—from the socialite in repose to the protesting Garveyite. Although mainstream photography scholarship treats Van Der Zee as an exception—that is, if he is acknowledged at all—there must be more, many, many more.

The 1920's were very special years for Black artists in the United States—particularly for the writers and painters who, unlike the musicians of that era, had not yet established themselves within a cultural continuum that was distinctly and affirmatively Afro-American. "We younger Negro artists who create now intend to express our individual dark-skinned selves without fear or shame."[9] This was Langston Hughes's proclamation in "The Negro Artist and the Racial Mountain." By the end of that decade, Black literary and visual artists had laid the foundation for an explicitly Afro-American aesthetic, one that reflected the sociohistorical conditions of the Black community's development and gave expression to the cultural traditions created and preserved in that process.

Let the blare of Negro jazz bands and the bellowing voice of Bessie Smith singing the blues penetrate the closed cars of the colored near-intellectuals until they listen and perhaps understand. Let Paul Robeson singing "Water Boy" and Rudolph Fisher writing about the streets of Harlem and Jean Toomer holding the heart of Georgia in his hands and Aaron Douglass drawing strange fantasies . . .[10]

And, we might add, James Van Der Zee capturing photographic images of Harlem, P. H. Polk preserving via the camera something of the historical import of Tuskegee Institute . . .

Then came the Great Crash of 1929, and the economic depression that brought misery to the entire population but whose impact was most fatal for the Afro-American masses, especially the agricultural workers of the South. Poor Black people appeared in the work of the Farm Security Administration photographers—Dorothea Lange, Ben Shahn, Carl Nydans, Walker Evans—whose documentation of rural life during the Depression years is of inestimable importance. Countless images of poverty in the United States have been preserved, yet Black people, like their white counterparts, were not simply poor. Their lives expressed far more than the "dignity despite poverty" often unintentionally captured in the photographs. Where are the other images—those of Black people organizing, struggling, fighting back as sharecroppers and tenant farmers in rural Alabama? As union militants in Detroit, for example, or as unemployed protesters in Chicago—and as people, real human beings? In short, as a maturing, complex community of oppressed people in relentless pursuit of a humane collective existence, a pursuit that continued throughout the 1940's and 1950's to the present time? If such images are to be unearthed, if new images of this sort are to be forged in substantial numbers, Afro-American photographers will have borne—and must continue to bear—the overwhelming burden of this responsibility.

The photography critic Gisele Freund has argued that the medium's importance is not only related to its capacity to develop as an art form, but also, and perhaps even more significantly, to ". . . its ability to shape our ideas, to influence our behavior and to define our society."[11] If racism is to be conquered in the United States, both in its institutional and attitudinal manifestations, then certainly Afro-American photographers must play a special role in the process of redefining the ideologically tainted imagery of their people. This process involves not only their own technical expertise, not only their aesthetic and social sensitivity, but also, in a very fundamental sense, the end of their socially imposed invisibility. Referring to a brilliant comtemporary photographer, A. D. Coleman wrote:

> It is little short of tragic that our prejudices should have deprived Roy De Carava of the wide audience he deserves, and deprived that audience of an artist with so much to reveal that they desperately need to know.[12]

Roy De Carava and how many more?

NOTES

1. Allon Schoener, ed., *Harlem on My Mind: Cultural Capital of Black America 1900–1968* (New York: Dell, 1979), p. 11.

2. A. D. Coleman, *Light Readings* (New York: Oxford University Press, 1979), p. 27.

3. Ibid., p. 16.

4. Beaumont Newhall, *The History of Photography* (New York: The Museum of Modern Art, 1982).

5. W.E.B. DuBois, *The Souls of Black Folk* (New York: New American Library, 1969), pp. 46–47.

6. David C. Driskell, *Two Centuries of Black American Art* (New York:

Alfred A. Knopf, Los Angeles County Museum of Art, 1976), p. 36.

7. W.E.B. DuBois, *Black Reconstruction in America* (New York: Meridian Books, 1964), p. 122.

8. Coleman, *op. cit.*, p. 17.

9. Langston Hughes, "The Negro Artist and the Racial Mountain" (first published in *The Nation*, June 23, 1926) in Williams and Harris, eds., *Amistad I* (New York: Vintage, 1970), p. 305.

10. Ibid., pp. 304–5.

11. Gisele Freund, *Photography and Society* (Boston: David R. Godine, 1980), p. 5.

12. Coleman, *op. cit.*, p. 28.

Brushstrokes
for Social Change:
The Art of Rupert Garcia

In the spring of 1978, a pioneering exhibit opened at the San Francisco Museum of Modern Art. While many of the people in attendance were schooled in the conventional ways of museum-going and art-viewing, a good number of those present were probably visiting a museum for the first time. Youngsters and seniors—indeed, entire families from Latino and other ethnic backgrounds—had made the trek to San Francisco's renowned fortress of artistic endeavor in order to pay tribute to a young Chicano who was rapidly emerging as one of the Bay Area's most brilliant artists. They danced to the music of mariachis, ceremoniously initiating the museum so that its walls might bear Rupert Garcia's images with the appropriate dignity of his ethnic heritage. Indeed, a new excitement pervaded the celebration. Not only had a young Chicano been invited to stage a one-person

—Originally published as preface to *Rupert Garcia* (Honolulu: Institute of Culture and Communications East-West Center, 1987), catalogue accompanying exhibition June 1–July 31, 1987.

show at San Francisco's most prestigious art museum, but the fact that his work contained overt manifestations of solidarity with the political struggles of oppressed peoples made Rupert Garcia's exhibit a tradition-shattering event.

I had known Rupert Garcia for some five years when I attended this opening, but I had been acquainted with his work even before our first meeting. While I was in jail awaiting trial on charges of murder, kidnapping, and conspiracy, my attorney brought one of his posters to my cell. It bore my portrait along with the slogan "*Libertad para los prisoneros politicos.*" Of the scores of posters produced during the two-year period of my imprisonment and trial, this was unquestionably among those that most acutely sensitized people to the fight for the freedom of political prisoners and particularly to the campaign for my own freedom.

In 1969, the University of California Board of Regents (of which then Governor Ronald Reagan was an active ex-officio member) fired me from my position as a professor of philosophy on allegations that my membership in the Communist party rendered me "undesirable" as a teacher. In the process of defending my right to teach, I became involved in efforts to prevent the fraudulent conviction of George Jackson, John Clutchette, and Fleeta Drumgo, who were charged with the murder of a Soledad prison guard in January 1970. During the summer of that year, Jonathan Jackson, George's younger brother, used weapons registered in my name—guns I had purchased for security purposes because of numerous anti-Communist and racist threats on my life—to initiate a prisoner revolt at the Marin County Courthouse in San Rafael, California. In the aftermath, I myself was charged with conspiracy and kidnapping, and with the murder of the judge killed during the confrontation. My only hope of escaping California's gas chamber resided in the people's movement that was being organized across the country and eventually on other continents as well.

As those who organized the National United Committee to Free Angela Davis and All Political Prisoners (NUCFAD) came to realize, the role of art in the campaign was indispensable, for it could frequently communicate our message far more forcefully than the usual flyers and speeches, important though those media were. With a persuasive simplicity, Rupert Garcia's *"Libertad para los prisoneros politicos"* placed a deep moral and political responsibility upon those who associated themselves with progressive causes. It was incumbent upon them to make an active contribution to the defense of those of us whose lives were threatened by the prevailing repression.

I made Rupert Garcia's personal acquaintance for the first time in September 1973. I remember the date because the recent overthrow of Salvador Allende and the Unidad popular government of Chile was being discussed at the event where we met. (Rupert later produced a moving piece entitled "Mexico, Chile, Soweto . . .") We spoke about his portrait of me and of its important presence within the campaign for my freedom. At that time, he showed me another poster reflecting the struggles of the period during which I had been incarcerated: *"Attica es Fascismo."* The message communicated by that slogan was inherent in the image itself—a symbolic skull captured the murderous assault on the prisoners ordered by then New York Governor Nelson Rockefeller in response to their demands for less crowded living conditions, better food and medical care, and, among other things, the freedom to read radical political literature.

Incorporating a recurring theme in Rupert Garcia's work, these two posters revealed the search for human freedom with the powerful visual impact so characteristic of his work as a whole.

There can be no mistake about the relationship between this artist's images and the real political struggles for the emancipation of oppressed people. The roots of his art can be discovered in an aesthetic tradition forged within the very heart of the Black and Chicano movements of the late 1960's. Indeed, some of his early works were produced in connection with the events surrounding the San Francisco State College Strike of 1968, which won the right to establish programs in Black and Chicano Studies as well as Native American and Asian-American Studies. During this period, Rupert created two posters inspired by the battles of Cesar Chavez and the United Farmworkers Union, and several portraits of Black Panther party members who had become victims of one of the most brutal waves of political repression the country has ever witnessed. And what did his portraits of Che Guevara and Emiliano Zapata symbolize if not the bonds of those movements with the worldwide rising of the downtrodden and oppressed?

Rupert Garcia has always had one obvious and overriding concern: the communication of human images that preserve our awareness of our racial and national heritages and of our people's collective struggles for freedom and dignity. Thus, many who may have been historically excluded from portraiture find their place in his work. And those who have offered contributions to our struggles who would otherwise be hidden behind the thick web of historical facts woven by orthodox historians are very much at home in the body of Rupert Garcia's work. The Reverend Ben Chavis, whose freedom was militantly demanded in the 1976 March on Raleigh, North Carolina, joins hands with Iñez Garcia, the victim of severe judicial punishment because she dared to fight back against the rapist who had assaulted her. A striking Mexican worker is assassinated, but Nelson Mandela, the imprisoned leader of the African National Congress of South Africa, perseveres, even as he suffers under the murderous repression of apartheid. In all of these images, a bold appeal is made to us who witness the work to carry on that very same legacy of human struggle.

While this artist's cultural heritage as a Chicano is a major theme in his life and work, this certainly does not prevent him from defining himself and his art as internationalist, with the aim of forging strong bonds between movements unfolding across the globe. From Mexico, he moves toward Chile and the Philippines, and toward Iran, South Africa, and Mozambique. If the internationalist dimension of his work is unmistakable, so is its explicit and successful pursuit of universality. Traditionally, the great majority of white critics, in approaching the work of racially oppressed visual and literary artists who explore the experiences and struggles of their peoples, have tended to dismiss it on the grounds that it is "provincial," or not sufficiently "universal." Critics of this type, whose attitudes have been thoroughly tainted by racism, have been frequently compelled, by the very strength of Rupert Garcia's work, to acknowledge within it a universality immersed in the visual concreteness of Third World peoples' cries for equality.

About the art-historical context of this work, there need be no speculation, for Rupert's portraiture preserves the images of many artists who have created and honed the aesthetic tradition within which he continues to work. Affirming his Chicano culture and his Mexican artistic heritage are the portraits of Diego Rivera, Frida Kahlo, Tamayo, Sizueiros, and Orozco. Images of the Communist painter Pablo Picasso, as well as the German revolutionary dramatic artist Berthold Brecht, emphasize the global character of the aesthetic tradition that places art in an unabashed relationship to progressive political struggle.

Rupert Garcia is not content with the process of image-making alone. He has sought to guarantee that other artists who work within his tradition might have the opportunity to pursue their work. That he was a founding member of San Francisco's Galería de la Raza is evidence of his commitment to the special cause of progressive artists, particularly those from racially and nationally oppressed communities. His work will undoubtedly furnish enduring inspiration for that cause.

ANGELA DAVIS was born and raised in Birmingham, Alabama. She graduated magna cum laude from Brandeis University and pursued graduate studies at the Goethe Intitute in Frankfurt and the University of California, San Diego. She has been a member of the Communist Party, U.S.A., since 1968 and has twice (in 1980 and 1984) run as its vice presidential candidate. Acquitted on conspiracy charges in 1970, after one of the most famous trials in U.S. history, Davis has emerged as an internationally regarded writer, scholar, lecturer, and fighter for human rights. She is a founder and co-chair of the National Alliance Against Racist and Political Repression and serves on the national board of directors of the National Political Congress of Black Women and on the board of the National Black Women's Health Project. She lives in California, where she teaches philosophy, aesthetics, and women's studies at San Francisco State University and the San Francisco Art Institute. Her previous books include *If They Come in the Morning: Voices of Resistance*; *Angela Davis: An Autobiography*; and *Women, Race & Class*.